Julia Goodfellow-Smith

111 Places in Cardiff That You Shouldn't Miss

emons:

Diolch i bobl Cymru am eich croeso cynnes.

Bibliographical information of the Deutsche Nationalbibliothek
The Deutsche Nationalbibliothek lists this publication in the Deutsche Nationalbibliografie; detailed bibliographical data are available on the internet at http://dnb.d-nb.de.

Cäcilienstraße 48, 50667 Köln
info@emons-verlag.de

Layout: Editorial Design & Art Direction, Conny Laue,
by Lübbeke | Naumann | Thoben
Maps: altancicek.design, www.altancicek.de
Basic cartographical information from Openstreetmap,

Edited by: Tania Taylor
Printing and binding: Grafisches Centrum Cuno, Calbe
Printed in Germany 2025
ISBN 978-3-7408-2465-5
First edition

Guidebooks for Locals & Experienced Travellers
Join us in uncovering new places around the world at
www.111places.com

Foreword

Cardiff has a gruesome and spectacular past, an awesome present and an exciting future unfolding every day.

People have lived here for thousands of years, leaving layers of history behind: Prehistoric people constructed hill forts; the Romans built a fort at the river crossing and started to drain and farm marshland along the Bristol Channel; the Normans built a castle on the site of the fort. The town grew, but the population was still small until the coal boom of the Industrial Revolution. At that point, Cardiff expanded rapidly, attracting migrants from across the world. Since then, it has become a city, a capital city and, more recently, a seat of government.

Over the last 200 years, Cardiff has changed beyond recognition. It is now a vibrant, multicultural city with a civic quarter that would rival that of any European capital. It has been at the forefront of scientific advances, such as Marconi's development of communication by radio, and societal changes, such as providing employment for those with disabilities. In this book, I convey some of this history through visits to quirky and unusual places.

But Cardiff is not just a city of the past. It is a city of the present, with many places where you can learn, have fun and relax. And it is a city of the future, with continued development in line with becoming an economically, socially and environmentally sustainable One Planet City.

With these 111 places, I aim to surprise, inspire and delight locals who already know Cardiff well and visitors experiencing it for the first time. I had swum around in Cardiff's waters a little before starting this book, and knew I would love writing it. Full immersion in those waters to research these 111 places has been fascinating and such fun! I hope you enjoy your exploration of Wales' capital city through the places and stories in this book as much as I have enjoyed unearthing them.

111 Places

Croeso i
Gorse

1 Aneurin 'Nye' Bevan Statue

Founder of the NHS

Free access to medical services at point of use has been a mainstay of UK society for so long that it's hard now to imagine life without the NHS. However, this great institution only came into being after World War II, thanks to the driving force of Nye Bevan.

Nye was one of 10 children, only five of whom reached adulthood. His father was a miner in Tredegar in the South Wales Valleys. As was often the way, Nye also became a miner after leaving school at 14. It was not long before he started to rail against the power held by the mine owners, and by the age of 19, he was head of the Miners' Lodge – the local National Union of Mineworkers organisation.

He was granted a bursary for the Central Labour College in London, where he studied economics, politics and history for two years before heading home. It seems that the mine owners were happy for him to have left and refused to employ him again on his return. But, they were not rid of him yet. After being unemployed for three years, he became a paid union official and led the local miners in the General Strike of 1926.

By 1929, he was spreading his wings beyond Tredegar and became the Labour MP for Ebbw Vale. He was unafraid to share his views on how things should be done and was a vocal opponent of both the Conservative government and the Labour opposition. Despite this, when Labour came to government in 1945, he was offered the position of Minister of Health.

As a child, he had seen how the Tredegar Medical Aid Society had provided free health care at point of use for the 95 per cent of local residents who made a regular financial contribution, and he proposed a similar scheme across the UK. The scheme was opposed by many people and organisations, including the British Medical Association, but he eventually got enough agreement for the NHS to be born just a few years later, in 1948.

Address Queen Street, Cardiff, CF10 2AF | **Getting there** Megabus to Cardiff North Road; bus 44, 45, 49, 50 to Castle Street; train to Cardiff Central | **Hours** Accessible 24 hours | **Tip** The Burger King nearby has a secret room upstairs with mahogany panels, mosaics and stained glass windows. The windows can be seen from street level.

2 Animal Wall

Cardiff's concrete jungle

The 3rd Marquess of Bute used the money his family had made from coal and shipping to renovate Cardiff Castle. He and his architect, William Burges, shared a love of animals, which is evident in the fantastical, naturalistic decoration of the castle that features animals in wood, glass and paintings. He even had clothes moths carved into his wardrobe!

Burges had a vision of extending the animal theme to the castle's exterior, allowing the people of Cardiff to see exotic animals that would otherwise have been unfamiliar to them. This vision was not realised until the 1890s, a few years after his death. Initially, a pair of lions holding the family shields flanked the castle entrance. They were joined by a lioness, polar bear, sea lion, wolf, a pair of apes and a hyena.

In the 1920s, the animal wall was moved to its current position to accommodate the widening of Castle Street. At the same time, the collection was enlarged to include a vulture, beaver, leopard, racoon, pelican, anteater and lynx. Although the sculptures we see now are bare stone, they were originally very different, with glass eyes and painted in realistic colours. While not as colourful as it once was, the animal wall has now been an educational visitor attraction for around a century.

Lord Bute did not only introduce decorative animals to the castle. He loved animals so much that he even had a hedgehog as a pet. He also introduced live beavers into the castle grounds, which extended into what is now Bute Park, hoping to re-establish an animal that was common when the castle was first built. Unfortunately, there are no longer beavers in Bute Park, although they have been successfully reintroduced in several rural areas of the UK. If you want to see these creatures in Cardiff now, your best bet is to head to the roof garden at the top of Bute Tower, where bronze beavers frolic around the fountain.

Address Castle Street, Cardiff, CF10 1SZ | Getting there Several buses to Cardiff Bridge; train to Cardiff Central | Hours Accessible 24 hours | Tip Behind the Animal Wall, Bute Park also has some animal sculptures.

3 Antarctic 100 Memorial

'I may be some time'

Captain Scott's ill-fated expedition to Antarctica, which left Cardiff in 1910, is best known for losing both the race to the South Pole and the lives of Scott and his men. It was a Norwegian team under Roald Amundsen who reached the South Pole first, so the Antarctic 100 Memorial makes an uncomfortable bedfellow with the Norwegian Church next door.

Scott's expedition was not the failure that we might think, though. There were several expeditions and scientific endeavours that were undertaken alongside the race to the pole. When the *Terra Nova* left Roath Dock, no one could have imagined the future value of the research that the scientists on board led. The scientific disciplines represented included zoology, glaciology, meteorology, physics, geology and biology.

Those on the expedition risked their lives to collect over 2,000 specimens of fossils, plants and animals, over 400 of which were new to science. The fossilised remains of *Glossopteris indica* showed that Antarctica had once been temperate enough to support vegetation. The known distribution of the same fossils around the southern hemisphere supported the theory that Antarctica was once connected to other continents and that, somehow, they had drifted apart.

Back in the early 20th century, few people had any idea about the impact that burning fossil fuels would have on our atmosphere, and yet the meteorological data collected is being used by today's climate scientists. It was of sufficient quality and collected over a long enough period that it is now used as a baseline against which to assess climate breakdown. Climate scientists are also comparing the photos taken on the expedition with the current situation to assess the impacts of climate breakdown.

Perhaps the *Terra Nova* Expedition should be remembered more for its contribution to science than the fate of five of the team.

Address Harbour Drive, Cardiff, CF10 4PA | Getting there Several buses to Mermaid Quay; train or tram to Cardiff Bay | Hours Accessible 24 hours | Tip There is a Scott of the Antarctic exhibition on the city side of the footpath across the barrage.

4 The Arcades

Shopping in comfort

The Industrial Revolution, in which Cardiff played a leading role, ushered in a new middle class with money to spend, and shopping became a recreational activity. Department stores started to thrive as a safe place for women to shop without a male escort. And then came the precursor to the shopping mall – arcades.

In the middle of the 19th century, slums blighted Cardiff town centre. The town had nearly 50 'courts', each housing up to 500 people. Multiple people shared each room, many households shared each privy, and communal water pumps were polluted with sewage. Given these living conditions, it is no surprise that in 1849, a cholera epidemic swept through the town, killing 383 people. Living conditions were so bad that a quarter of all Cardiff children did not live to see their first birthday. Eventually, all the slums were cleared. Between The Hayes and St Mary's Street, they were replaced by smart new buildings with shops facing each other across a walkway. Iron trellises supporting a glass roof spanned the gap, providing a clean and comfortable shopping environment, whatever the weather. After all, shopping was now to be enjoyed, not simply endured.

The first arcade in Cardiff was the Royal Arcade, opened in 1858. A proliferation followed, including the Morgan Arcade, the Castle Arcade and the Wyndham Arcade, all of which remain open. Cardiff became known as the 'City of Arcades'.

These extraordinary shopping streets remain a critical part of life in Cardiff, with seven of the Victorian and Edwardian arcades continuing to offer a unique shopping experience in Cardiff city centre. Resisting the march towards globalisation, homogenisation and the death of the high street, the arcades provide Cardiffians with access to over 100 independent stores, eateries and drinking establishments, as well as a few well-known brands.

Address Across Cardiff City Centre, www.thecityofarcades.com | Getting there Train to Cardiff Central | Hours See individual websites for hours | Tip If you fancy some refreshments in the fresh air when you've finished shopping, head to Church Street, where there is a plethora of restaurants with outdoor seating.

5 Betty Campbell Monument

Mounting the insurmountable

It was not until 2021 that the people of Wales were treated to their first monumental statue of a Welsh woman. That woman was Betty Campbell, who has made history twice – once as a headteacher determined to achieve change, and again as a larger-than-life statue.

Betty Campbell was a working-class Black girl who grew up in Tiger Bay. Her dad was killed in World War II, and her mum struggled to manage financially afterwards. However, Betty loved to study and succeeded in securing a scholarship to a high school. Most of the other pupils were white and middle class. The teachers, too. Despite being a good student, when she expressed an interest in becoming a teacher herself, one of the teachers told her that 'the problems would be insurmountable'.

First, she cried. Then, she set out to prove them wrong. In her mid-twenties, she heard that Cardiff Teacher Training College would accept female students for the first time. She applied and was one of six in the first cohort of female students. Her teaching career started at Llanrumney, but it was not long before she was back at Mount Stuart Primary School, where she worked for decades, first as a teacher and then as headteacher – the first Black headteacher in Wales. She added Black history into the school's curriculum so that her pupils could understand more about their own backgrounds. Later, she helped bring Black History Month to the UK to ensure that there is at least one period each year when pupils learn about Black people's roles in our history.

Betty Campbell's influence did not end there, with positions on the Home Office's Race Advisory Committee and the Commission for Racial Equality. And now, she continues to influence in a monumental way, reminding all who see her statue of the value of learning, childhood, a multicultural society, and of the sort of world we want to inhabit.

Address Central Square, Cardiff, CF10 1PN | Getting there Several buses to Wood Street; train to Cardiff Central | Hours Accessible 24 hours | Tip There are several statues of unnamed women in Cardiff, including one on St Mary's Street and another outside the One Kingsway building.

6 Billy the Seal

Sealed with a myth

An urban myth says that Billy the Seal was caught in trawler nets in 1912 and transferred to Victoria Park to live there. However, the park records tell a different story.

The tale starts in 1900 when the parks committee approved a small building called *The Aviary* to house a zoo. It wasn't long before ships' captains began to bring gifts from around the world to Cardiff for the newly created zoo. These included monkeys, gazelles, owls, a mongoose and crocodiles. It must have been quite a spectacle.

By 1908, the zoo held 58 birds and mammals, and work was started to build new accommodation to house them all. In 1915, despite the challenges created by World War I, Councillor H. M. Thompson donated Billy the Seal to the zoo, and a new lake was provided to house him. During the war, the zoo agreed to house several regiments' mascots.

First, three goats arrived, the mascots of the 11th Welsh Regiment (Cardiff Pals) and the 2/5 Battalion, Welsh Regiment. In May 1919, the zoo accepted Billy the Goat, the mascot of the 38th Heavy Battery, Royal Garrison Artillery, along with a raven, which was also the mascot of one of the battalions of the Welsh Regiment. Now there were two Billys.

Two other seals presented to the zoo died shortly after they arrived, possibly because they were housed in freshwater lakes. However, this did not seem to faze Billy, who lived there for 24 years until she died in 1939. She? Yes! A post-mortem revealed that Billy was, in fact, a female seal. The zoo closed two years later when the land was needed for the World War II Dig For Victory campaign. The remaining animals were sold. Some suggest they went to Bristol Zoo, but there is no record of Bristol Zoo receiving them.

A statue of Billy perched on a rock was erected in the park in 1997 to celebrate the love that the people of Cardiff had for its namesake and the park's centenary.

Address Victoria Park, Cardiff, CF5 1JN | Getting there Bus 2 City Circle, 32, 96 to Victoria Park; on-road parking nearby (it gets busy) | Hours Daily 7.30am–30 minutes before sunset | Tip Victoria Park is also home to a brilliant splash-pad wet-play area for children (www.outdoorcardiff.com/parks).

7 Blackfriars Priory

From black cloaks to bedding plants

When the 3rd Marquess of Bute inherited Cardiff Castle and its surrounding parkland, he had a good old poke around. While re-landscaping the castle, he discovered the remains of the walls of a Roman fort buried below Norman earthworks. This led to his ambitious restoration of the fort and the long, straight walls surrounding the castle today.

He wasn't quite as ambitious with the remains of the priory he unearthed in Bute Park. The site was excavated to reveal the medieval floorplan, but instead of rebuilding to its full height as he did with the Roman fort, a dozen or so layers of bricks were built up to show the shape of the buildings. Bedding plants were added to the top, in keeping with the rest of the park he was creating. He did, however, lay replica medieval tiles over the floor of the church. These have now been moved to the tea rooms at the West Gate. As he did with the Roman walls at the castle, Lord Bute provided a visual representation of where the old walls met the new – black and yellow bricks were placed over actual medieval remains, and red ones where walls were thought to have been. A model of the priory stands to one side of the site, representing how it once looked. Today's formal planting is in an area once surrounded by cloisters, and the circular bed is where a fountain once stood.

During Lord Bute's excavations, a seal associated with Pope Innocent IV was found. He was Pope between 1243 and 1254, which helps to date the priory. The name 'Blackfriar' might conjure images of foreboding, but the name was given purely because it was a Dominican priory and Dominican monks wear black cloaks over their white habits. When Henry VIII broke with the church in Rome and created his own church, he dissolved Catholic religious houses, including this one. The priory had stood for almost 300 years, but seven friars signed a deed of surrender, and the buildings were quickly demolished.

Address Bute Park, Cardiff, CF10 3RB | Getting there Several buses to Cardiff Bridge; train to Cardiff Central; head into park from tea rooms on Castle Street – remains are on left after 230 metres | Hours Accessible 24 hours | Tip Friary Gardens on Kingsway are about 450 metres to the east and offer an oasis of formal planting amid tall buildings and busy roads. These are named after the Franciscan order of monks, who wore grey cloaks and also had a friary nearby.

8 Bomb Site, Stockland Street

Baked-in memory

An observant passerby will notice that the building on the corner of Stockland Street and Corporation Road does not match the Victorian design of the neighbouring houses. This is because this rather unprepossessing building has a story to tell.

During World War II, the fact that Cardiff was an important coal port for the Allied forces did not escape the Germans' attention, and the city became a target for bombing raids. The most concerted happened between 1940 and 1941, and the worst was on 2 January, 1941. That night, the German bombers made the most of the full moon and blitzed the city for 10 hours. Residents hunkered down in basements and bomb shelters, listening to hour after hour of planes flying overhead and the subsequent explosions, as parts of their city were flattened.

Some people sheltered in the basement bunker below Hollyman Brothers Bakery, hoping that they and others would be safe. Unfortunately, this was not to be the case. One of the bombs dropped through the house and into the cellar before exploding and killing all 32 who were sheltering there.

They were not the only unlucky ones that night – over 150 people lost their lives and more than 400 were injured. Around 350 homes were also destroyed or damaged beyond repair.

Of course, there are also stories of good luck associated with the Cardiff Blitz. For example, a flag that the 4th Cardiff Scouts had given to Captain Scott to take to Antarctica seems to be charmed. First, it made it back from Antarctica. Then, when the hall it was displayed in was destroyed in the blitz, it was found unscathed in the rubble. Since then, its good luck has persisted, having survived both a flood and a fire before being safely stored in Amgueddfa Cymru, the national museum.

The building on the corner of Stockland Street and Corporation Road was rebuilt after the war, and even operated as a bakery again for a while.

Address 64 Corporation Road, Cardiff, CF11 7AW | Getting there Several buses to Stockland Street; on-street parking nearby | Hours Viewable from the outside only | Tip From Corporation Road, turn along Llanbradach Street for a riverside stroll in Taff Embankment Park.

9 The Bone Yard

Containers of creativity

The road leading to the Bone Yard passes under a railway bridge and then between the railway and industrial units. Vehicles are parked along one side, litter blows down the street, and the whole area emits an air of unloved grittiness. It is not a promising entrance. However, once you turn into the Bone Yard itself, the industrial grittiness becomes cared for, with a more welcoming and friendly air.

Picnic tables cluster together in front of a shiny counter serving an interesting array of hot and cold food and drinks, including alcohol. Painted shipping containers are dotted around the edges of the yard, housing a variety of craftspeople. Each container accommodates a small studio, workshop or retail space, providing just enough room for small artisan businesses to flourish. This is a place to come to try out crafts such as painting pottery, crochet and woodwork, or simply to buy that quirky, handmade gift directly from the craftsperson who made it, and settle down for lunch with friends or family.

The Bone Yard was established to transform an unused and unloved industrial site into a thriving ecosystem for small businesses, artists and artisans. And it has succeeded. The design lets visitors see at a glance what opportunities there are and encourages them to linger and visit several of the makers' units. The middle of the yard is kept clear, allowing people to congregate and providing space for community events.

In a world of homogenised high streets and corporate-dominated spaces, the Bone Yard allows Cardiff's creatives to flourish. It serves as a cultural hub and community space. It also encourages visitors to the area and invites them to create and explore their potential. The Bone Yard proves that with vision and community support, even the most unlikely and unlovely places can be transformed into vibrant centres of art, craft and commerce.

Address Paper Mill Road, Cardiff, CF11 8DH, www.shippingcontainerstudios.co.uk, jodie@cranejewellery.co.uk | Getting there Train to Waun-Gron Park; several buses to Windway Road | Hours See website for current information on visiting | Tip Cardiff Christmas Market also allows you to meet and buy directly from artists and creators (www.cardiffchristmasmarket.com).

10 Bullring

Commonplace cruelty

In medieval times, cruelty was a way of life. Beating was seen as a legitimate form of training, so wives suffered at the hands of their husbands, children at the hands of their parents and dogs at the hands of their owners. Criminals were often treated particularly harshly, the severity of punishment increasing in line with the nature of the crime. For those crimes considered most heinous, techniques were developed so people could be disembowelled and kept alive to watch their innards being burnt, before they were hanged to death.

Even children were taught to be cruel. Alongside the traditional games you would recognise today, favourite pastimes included cock-fighting and cock-baiting. For the latter, the cocks were tied up and had stones thrown at them. The child who made the killing shot got to take the cock home for dinner.

Adult entertainment was on a grander scale, with baiting that involved larger animals, such as bulls. And the junction of Duke Street and Queen Street is the site of Cardiff's own medieval bullring, now long gone. Bulls were chained to posts or constrained in a pit while fighting dogs attacked them. To make this even more 'entertaining', pepper was blown up the bull's nose. This would enrage the animal, making it more likely that the attacking dogs would be gored or thrown into the air. Each participant would pay for their dog to take part, gaining points each time it bit the bull's nose. A prize was awarded for the winning dog, and bystanders would place bets on the outcome.

It was not until the turn of the 19th century that people started to become concerned about cruelty to animals, and animal baiting was made illegal. Although bear- and bull-baiting are no longer practised in British towns and cities, other forms of the 'sport' were driven underground. Clandestine badger-baiting – and prosecutions – continued into the 21st century, some 200 years after it was made illegal.

Address Duke Street, Cardiff, CF10 1AY | **Getting there** Bus 44, 45, 49 or 50 to Castle Street; train to Cardiff Central | **Hours** Accessible 24 hours | **Tip** The Rummer Tavern on Duke Street was established in 1713, so it is likely that some of those involved in bull-baiting were customers.

11 Bute Family Mausoleum

Sacred transitions

Shortly after the Norman invasion, Lord Robert Fitzhamon founded a small, whitewashed chapel in Roath. It was run by Tewkesbury Abbey, which provided clergy, wine and wax in exchange for tithes.

It remained as nothing more than a hamlet's chapel until 1792, when the 1st Marquess of Bute bought the land on which it stood. When his wife died in 1800, he built a mausoleum here for his family, which had space for 48 tombs. He was clearly expecting the Butes to have a long and illustrious future here in Cardiff. His grandson, the 3rd Marquess of Bute, was orphaned as a young child. When he reached the age of 21, he commissioned a local architect, John Pritchard, to build a Gothic church to replace the simple chapel. When the church opened in 1870, it had no spire or tower, but was highly regarded for its fine, highly decorated interior.

Ten years later, the 3rd Marquess arranged for the mausoleum to be rebuilt and incorporated into the church. He and his family were now Roman Catholics, so there would be no need for any additional tombs in this Protestant place of worship.

The mausoleum has a brick vaulted ceiling above multicoloured stone pillars with stone carvings. A gold mosaic of Christ in Majesty, flanked by a pair of angels, looks down on the nine members of the Bute family who lie here. They're sealed in triple coffins placed in polished red granite tombs, which are grand but plain. Although impressive, they give no hint of the flights of fancy that the 3rd Marquess incorporated into his decoration of the castle.

In 1926, the tower was added as a war memorial, and in 1952, a new stained glass window was installed to replace the one that was lost to bombing in World War II. The church is still used for worship and is open weekly to visitors. Once a year, the church offers full guided tours and, for the intrepid, the opportunity to climb the tower.

Address St Margaret's Church, Waterloo Road, Cardiff, CF23 5AQ, +44 (0) 292 048 7854, www.roath.org.uk/stmargaret | Getting there Bus 1 or 2 to Timbers Square or 30, 44 or 45 to Stacey Road | Hours Wed 10.30am; full church tour during Heritage Open Doors weekend in September | Tip Neighbouring Waterloo Gardens offer a delightful place to sit and contemplate life, or go for a stroll by Roath Brook.

12 Bute Street Railway Station

Standing strong

At the height of the coal boom in the South Wales valleys, as many as nine million tonnes of coal and coke were shipped from Cardiff docks per year. Transporting the coal from mines to ports provided a logistical challenge as roads were of poor quality, vehicles were slow and coal was heavy. The challenge was met by the clever engineers who developed the steam locomotive and railways. This led to the construction of the Taff Vale Railway from 1836, linking the Valleys with Cardiff. The main line was only 24 miles long, but there were 23 branch lines and over 124 miles of rail network in total. Tracks snaked up each of the valleys, joining them to Cardiff and through Cowbridge to Aberthaw, providing transportation for a burgeoning population of workers as well as coal.

The headquarters of the Taff Vale Railway Company were built between 1842 and 1843 at Cardiff Docks station on Bute Street. The railway thrived until the 20th century, when the coal fields and mining industry began to decline, thanks at least in part to the world's naval and merchant ships, and then railways, switching to oil-fired engines. From the 1920s, facilities on the Taff Vale Railway started to close.

Once the railway company vacated the building, it was used as a gallery in the Welsh Industrial and Maritime Museum to showcase trains. Then it became the headquarters of Butetown Historic Railway Society, which ran steam trains for tourists. In 1997, plans for the Cardiff Bay development did not include the running of steam trains – instead, electric tram-trains will operate between the bay and the city centre. The railway society moved to Barry and the building became empty and then derelict, threatening its status as 'one of the earliest locomotive railway buildings still standing'. Since then, it has been renovated and will hopefully remain standing for many more decades or centuries to come.

Address Platform, Hemingway Road, Cardiff, CF10 5LS | Getting there Train to Cardiff Bay station; bus 1 to Cardiff Bay Station | Hours Viewable from the outside only | Tip Head directly east to the Red Dragon Centre for cinema, bowling and restaurants (www.thereddragoncentre.co.uk).

13 Bute West Dock Basin

High-stakes stress

The Butes were a wealthy Scottish family who came to own land in South Wales through marriage in 1766. This included areas that had rich coal deposits, and a strip between Cardiff and the sea. When the world started to need coal to power the Industrial Revolution, the 2nd Marquess of Bute was therefore in pole position to exploit those resources.

Because of his immense wealth, he decided not to create financial partnerships to build the dock as landowners elsewhere did. However, this insistence was almost his downfall. He had to mortgage some of his land to borrow the money he needed, and the dock was not immediately successful. It opened in 1839 to a fanfare, and then promptly had to close for three years while shoddy workmanship was repaired. Once reopened, the dock did thrive, but it seems that the 2nd Marquess remained anxious about the size of his investment. He died in 1848 from a heart attack at the tender age of 54. At that point, the 3rd Marquess was only a boy, and the estate was managed by trustees.

By 1849, despite being over three times the size of the Newport docks, West Bute Dock was reaching capacity. The trustees invested again, and East Dock was partially opened in 1855. Ships were increasing in size so quickly that parts of West Dock were already becoming obsolete, so the trustees wanted to build more docks to accommodate the larger ships. However, they came across a significant stumbling block – Parliament refused to grant them permission while the 3rd Marquess remained a minor. That marked the end of the Bute family's monopoly on shipping from this area, as it opened the door for docks to be built at Penarth and Barry.

Bute West Dock has long since been infilled. However, the oval shape of the basin at the entrance to the dock is reflected in the outline of Roald Dahl Plass, picked out with a series of tall pillars.

Address Roald Dahl Plass, Cardiff, CF10 4PZ | Getting there Train to Cardiff Bay; Baycar 6 to Millennium Centre; bus 1, 8 or X2 to Mermaid Quay | Hours Accessible 24 hours | Tip Roath Basin, about 250 metres to the southeast and leading to Roath Dock, is a larger version of the Bute West Dock Basin, and still contains water.

14 By Water and Fire

Cardiff's dual heritage

The Bute Docks Company coat of arms adorns the outside of the iconic red brick Pierhead building in terracotta. The motto tells the story of the rise of Cardiff from a small town of 2,000 to a busy port 10 times that size: *WRTH DDWR A THAN – By water and fire.*

It was the 2nd Marquess of Bute who developed the infrastructure to transport coal from his mines in South Wales to the port in Cardiff and on to the rest of the world. In doing so, he transformed the fortunes and culture of the area and, it could be argued, the entire world.

Coal was the 'fire' element of the coat of arms; it was providing the energy for the Industrial Revolution, being burned in ships and locomotives to speed up transportation, in furnaces to create heat for industry, and, ultimately, in power stations to generate electricity.

Shipping was the 'water' element of the coat of arms, as coal was transported around the world. In 1896, the year before the Pierhead was opened, nearly 16 million tonnes of coal were exported through the Port of Cardiff (which included the docks at Barry and Penarth).

The barrage was not built across Cardiff Bay for another century – when the Pierhead was built, the docks were surrounded by mudflats most of the time, which meant that shipping was entirely dependent on the tides. The clocks were a visible reminder of the importance of working fast and being ready for the next high water.

The flamboyant French Gothic style of the Pierhead was fashionable at the time. It was prominent because of its size and design – and the startling red bricks and terracotta that were transported all the way from North Wales. It exudes confidence, although no one would have predicted that the coal boom would only last a few more decades, that the building would outlive the docks, or that it would become part of the estate for a Welsh government. How fortunes can turn, ebbing and flowing like the tide.

Address The Pierhead, Cardiff Bay, Cardiff, CF10 4PZ, +44 (0) 300 200 6565, www.senedd.wales | Getting there Baycar 6; bus 7 or 8 to Pierhead Street; train to Cardiff Bay | Hours Mon–Fri 9am–4.30pm, Sat & bank holidays 10.30am–4.30pm | Tip The Pierhead stands at one end of Roald Dahl Plass, a public plaza that often hosts concerts or events, including the Cardiff Food and Drink Festival early in July.

15 Caerau Fort

Six thousand years of history

During the early Stone Age, the residents of South Wales were nomadic hunter-gatherers. It was not until they started farming in the Neolithic period (from Greek words for 'new' and 'stone' – the 'New Stone' Age) that they started to build enclosures and forts.

Around 6,000 years ago, the first structure to be built on the hill at Caerau was a 'causewayed enclosure'. This was created by digging ditches up to three metres deep and using the spoil to create banks. The ditches were roughly rectangular, with a causeway between each. It is the causeways that make archaeologists think that these enclosures were not defensive. No evidence of settlements has been found within these enclosures, either. Rather, it is thought that they were used as a place for the first farmers to gather, conduct business, celebrate and worship. This type of enclosure is common across southern England, and more are now being discovered in Wales. Here, an excavation revealed stone axes, flint tools and Neolithic pottery buried in the ditches.

In the Bronze Age, around 2,600 years ago, a similar method of digging ditches and building banks was used to create a larger defensive hill fort on the same site, but without the causeways. It is thought that this was a major centre of power for the area.

There is no evidence of Roman occupation of the site, but when the Normans arrived around 1,000 years ago, they could see its potential. They used the site for a church and a small castle. The remains of St Mary's Church, which dates from around 1260, stand in an oval enclosure. It was renovated in 1885 and closed in 1957. Since then, it has been restored and abandoned again, allowing it to become the ruin we see today. It is thought that the oval ring next to the church is the remains of an unregistered Norman castle, probably belonging to the Bishop of Llandaff, and the home of a Norman nobleman and his family.

Address Church Road, Caerau, Cardiff, CF5 5LQ, www.caerheritage.org | Getting there Bus 17 to Home Guard Club or 18 to Hoel-y-Gaer | Hours Accessible 24 hours | Tip If you'd like to help look after Caerau Fort, Love our Hillfort volunteers meet at the CAER Heritage Centre on Church Road at 10am every Wednesday for two hours.

16 Capel I Bawb

A healthy love of reading

The earliest libraries were not repositories of learning or stories. These first libraries were repositories of business deals, recorded on clay tablets that were carved while still damp, then dried to provide a permanent record. Later, scrolls made from papyrus or parchment replaced the clay tablets, and later again, bound books took their place.

In medieval times in the UK, the only libraries were in monasteries. It might take a monk six months to copy a book, so they were immensely expensive to produce. This resulted in most books being chained to the shelves so they weren't stolen, although with a hefty enough deposit, it was possible to borrow them to make copies. Copyright protections for writers had not yet come into being!

In 1850, the Public Libraries Act allowed local authorities in the UK to raise taxes to pay for public libraries. The intention behind these libraries was not education or entertainment, but to offer an alternative activity to working-class people so they would spend more time reading and less time boozing.

These days, libraries like Capel I Bawb serve a broader function in society. They enable everyone, no matter how rich or poor, to access and read a broad range of books, whether for research, learning or pure enjoyment. In keeping with the times, they also offer the opportunity to borrow an ebook or audiobook free of charge. Rather than the hushed spaces of old, and despite its location in what was the hospital chapel, this library offers a social space among the books, where people can meet and chat in the café. Here at Capel I Bawb, or 'Chapel for All' in English, hospital staff, visitors and locals can sit in the glow from the 1950s stained glass window depicting Christ on the Sea of Galilee, enjoy a cup of tea and lose themselves in a book or conversation. Books are not chained to the shelves, and a deposit is not needed to borrow one!

Address Cardiff Royal Infirmary, Glossop Road, Cardiff, CF24 0JT, www.cardiffhubs.co.uk/hub/capel-i-bawb | Getting there Several buses to Infirmary; train to Cardiff Queen Street | Hours Mon–Fri 7am–2pm (staff available from 10.30am) | Tip For something a little stronger or more substantial to go with your reading, The Ernest Willows Wetherspoons pub is a short walk to the north on City Road.

17 Cardiff Bay Barrage

The price and prize of progress

The barrage across Cardiff Bay was built at the turn of the 21st century to create an attractive waterfront rather than mudflats that were only covered for a few hours each day. Blocking rivers can be devastating to local wildlife, as muddy banks full of intertidal organisms become permanently submerged and migrating fish are confronted with an insurmountable barrier between them and their spawning grounds.

Since the 18th century, engineers have been working on a solution to the fish-migration issue. The Cardiff Bay Barrage uses the most popular version of a fish pass – a 'ladder'. This is a series of stepped pools that allows fish to jump up from the bay to the river, one step at a time. The trick is to make the steps just the right size, with enough water flow to attract the fish but not so much that climbing the ladder exhausts them.

The next challenge is to keep the fish alive once they reach the bay. Seawater holds less oxygen than freshwater, and because it's also heavier, it can get trapped behind the barrier. This has been tackled in several ways, including sluice gates that are raised to stop the ingress of seawater (although some still enters through the locks) and an aeration system that sends bubbles up through the water, mixing the salt and freshwater and adding oxygen.

No real solution has yet been found to the damage caused by permanently submerging mudflats, but some of the environmental losses have been offset with the wetlands reserve within the bay and investment in the wetlands at Nash, further up the Bristol Channel. There have also been social gains. Not only does Cardiff have a waterfront that attracts people to live here as well as visitors, but it also has a huge lake with marinas and sport and leisure facilities, and a lovely walk between Cardiff and Penarth that avoids the traffic-heavy river crossings further inland.

Address Penarth, Cardiff, CF64 1TP | Getting there Bus 305 to Barrage | Hours Accessible 24 hours | Tip The harbour wall is a great place to watch boats entering or leaving the bay through the locks. The pink building on stilts was built to give sailing-race organisers a good view of boats in the estuary.

18 Cardiff Bay Wetlands Reserve

A city sanctuary

When the intention to place a barrage across Cardiff Bay was announced, there was uproar in the conservation world. The mudflats that characterised the bay might not have been very sightly but they provided a home to a huge diversity of animals and birds.

As is evident from Cardiff's modern waterfront, the development went ahead. But some concessions were made to nature, and one of these was the formation of the Cardiff Bay Wetlands Reserve. This eight-hectare freshwater reserve in no way makes up for the 150 hectares of intertidal mudflats that were lost but it does at least provide a valuable habitat for wildlife, and people in its own way.

Much of the reserve is only hinted at through small gaps in the reeds. There are pools, islands and a long canal-like reen running through the reed beds. This provides a perfect habitat for several species of warbler and reed buntings. Small fish have nurseries protected by the reeds, but when they stray out of the protected zone, they instantly become attractive to herons and kingfishers hunting for their dinner.

Follow the boardwalk out into the bay, and you are likely to see swans, coots and great crested grebes – and a boom set up to keep litter out. Under the water, a gravel barrier protects the reserve and its wildlife from waves, like a reef on a tropical island. The views past moored leisure boats, across the bay to the barrage and Penarth Marina, could even make you think you are in the tropics on a sunny day. Less so when the grey clouds provide a low blanket of drizzle!

For a closer look at the wildlife, head towards the Victorian houses to the northwest of the site, where a platform leads to the edge of a lily pond. There is always something going on here, whether it's the ducks heading your way hoping for a titbit or fish swimming in the shallows.

Address Windsor Esplanade, Cardiff, CF10 5BG | Getting there Bus X2 to Stuart Street; train to Cardiff Bay (15-minute walk) | Hours Accessible 24 hours | Tip For a longer walk, take the 10-kilometre Cardiff Bay Trail, which runs around the whole bay (www.outdoorcardiff.com/walks/cardiff-bay-trail).

19_Cardiff Castle

The only rebuilt Roman fort in Britain

Cardiff Castle may be best known for its lavish interiors, created in the late 1800s by the 3rd Marquess of Bute and his architect, William Burges. The decoration is exquisite if a little gaudy by today's standards, and the tour is highly recommended.

When Lord Bute was remodelling the landscape around the castle, the groundworkers discovered a stone wall in what they had thought were Norman earth banks. Further investigation revealed the remains of a Roman fort. On discovering the remains, Bute decided to rebuild the Roman walls. He replicated the original to the best of his knowledge, except for the addition of a gallery in which he could exercise during inclement weather. He stipulated that the new walls should be distinguishable from the old, so a layer of red sandstone was added between the two. This can be seen in places along the outer wall of today's castle.

Ongoing archaeological work has now identified this as the final of four Roman forts on this site, at the lowest crossing point of the River Taff. All were square, which was typical, and the first three were wooden. The first was the biggest, as it needed to house a large army during the Roman invasion. The following two were smaller, built during a period of relative peace. The stone fort that replaced them was probably constructed in the final period of Roman rule when the empire was failing and the site was vulnerable to attack. Archaeological finds of pots that once contained oils and wines indicate that goods were consumed here from across the empire.

Between the Romans and the Victorians, the site was used by the Normans when they invaded Wales. Their legacy includes the artificial hill in the centre of the castle, known as a motte, with a stone keep on top. The castle also saw action in the British Civil Wars, and the gallery in the rebuilt Roman walls was used as a bomb shelter during World War II.

Address Castle Street, Cardiff, CF10 3RB, +44 (0) 292 087 8100, www.cardiffcastle.com | Getting there Several buses to Kingsway or Castle Street; train to Cardiff Central | Hours See website for seasonal hours | Tip There was once a Roman villa in Trelai Park. The site has been covered over, with the area marked by long grass (www.outdoorcardiff.com/parks).

20 Cardiff City Mental Hospital

A trailblazer in psychiatric care

In the early 20th century, all sorts of people were treated or incarcerated in 'lunatic asylums'. Unmarried mothers (and not fathers) were treated for moral imbecility, and masturbatory insanity was considered a form of lunacy. The advanced stages of syphilis were known as 'paralysis of the insane' and treated by giving patients malaria, so their high temperature would kill the offending parasite. Thank goodness that things have moved on in terms of how we think of mental illness and how it is treated.

It seems that a great deal of thanks should be directed to Dr Goodall, the hospital's first medical director. He immediately changed the name from Cardiff City Asylum to Cardiff City Mental Hospital. The hospital offered cutting-edge treatment for its patients, and the medical staff were at the forefront of research into treatment for shellshock (now known as post-traumatic stress disorder) in World War I.

After the war, the hospital continued to be a leading light. Occupational therapy was a new discipline when the hospital became an early adopter and employed Sister Patricia Sunderland, who became the first in the UK to publish a paper on this new treatment option.

Because patients lived here, the site had a dance hall, church, bandstand and summer house, as well as treatment and research areas. The tower had a generator at ground level with a water tank above. A farm provided patients with an activity that was good for their physical and mental health, as well as supplying food for the kitchens.

Most patients were there voluntarily and could have contact with people from the wider community. One of the failures of institutions like this was seen as the way patients became dependent on them and found it hard to leave, which is one of the reasons that care is now provided in the community, where possible.

Address Park Road, Cardiff, CF14 7BF | Getting there Bus 21, 23 or 136 to Hospital; train to Coryton | Hours Viewable from the outside only | Tip Mind Cymru supports people in Wales with mental-health problems. You can visit their shop at 338 Cowbridge Road East to support their work (www.mind.org.uk).

21 Cardiff Gaol

Dic Penderyn's downfall

Castles were historically the home of a city's gaol, which was also the case in Cardiff. However, in the 16th century, the growth of the prison population meant that the castle was no longer big enough, and a purpose-built gaol was constructed in the city centre. It remained in use until the 19th century, when it suffered from the same issue of overcrowding: in 1857, there were 152 prisoners in a facility designed to accommodate 60.

During this period, punishment could be more severe than today, and capital punishment was still legal. Sentences meted out included death by burning, boiling, drowning or being hung, drawn and quartered. However, some of the upper classes were pardoned for even the most murderous of crimes. For lesser offences, ordinary people were flogged, branded or shamed in the stocks.

Industrialisation and poverty in rural areas caused many people to move from the countryside to the Glamorgan valleys in search of work. The work was dangerous, wages were low and prices were high. Understandably, this led to antagonism between the mine and mill owners and the endangered and impoverished workers. This came to a head in June 1831 when disenfranchised workers destroyed the building in Merthyr in which the records of their debts were held. A heavy-handed response by the authorities led to riots in which 20 people lost their lives. Dic Penderyn (Richard Lewis) was one of the leaders of the riots and was accused of wounding one of the troops sent in to quell the action. Although he claimed he was innocent, he lost his case and was one of those executed near what is now the St Mary's Street entrance to the market. His final words were reportedly 'Oh Lord, here is iniquity'.

In the 19th century alone, a further eighteen men and one woman were hanged on this spot – a chilling part of Cardiff's past, gladly now consigned to history.

Address Cardiff Market, St Mary Street, Cardiff, CF10 1AT | Getting there Several buses to Westgate Street bus station; train to Cardiff Central | Hours Plaque accessible 24 hours | Tip The celebrity Pizza Boys have a pizza place in the market (www.ffwrnes.co.uk).

22 Cardiff International White Water

Rapids on request

Adrenaline seekers love the challenge of white water canoeing, and crowds love the spectacle of competitors trying to navigate such powerful forces. Canoe slalom was designed to replicate the thrills and spills of ski slalom by giving competitors gates through which they must pass, when the water might have other ideas. Canoe slalom can be done in kayaks (boats with an enclosed cockpit that are propelled with a double-bladed paddle) or canoes (boats with an open cockpit that are propelled with a single-bladed paddle). Canoe slalom has been an Olympic sport since 1992, but at the time, there were no on-demand white water centres in the UK. And our rivers have an unpredictable flow, which made training challenging.

Cardiff International White Water was created at the same time as the barrage was built and the bay became a lagoon. An Olympic-standard course was constructed, with powerful pumps to provide water on demand. This means the flow is predictable and adjustable to suit the participants, making it ideal for slalom canoeists at all levels to train here. However, you do not need to be a dedicated competitor to enjoy these facilities. White water rafting and tubing both offer visitors with no experience a chance to feel the excitement of riding the rapids and avoiding obstacles where they can.

Although perhaps not the best craft to use on white water, the centre also offers an opportunity for people to use paddleboards. A small flat area of still water below the rapids provides the perfect space for a lesson before launching out into the bay proper, where there is plenty to explore. The same area is used for supervised wild swimming.

Continuing the white water theme inside, the centre also has an indoor wave, where you can practise surfing or bodyboarding.

Address Watkiss Way, Cardiff, CF11 0SY, +44 (0) 292 082 9970, www.ciww.com, info@ciww.com | **Getting there** Bus 305 or 9 to Cardiff Ice Rink, Olympian Drive or Watkiss Way | **Hours** Advance booking required – check website for details | **Tip** Coffi Co Bayscape café is at the far end of the watercourse if you fancy refreshments after your white-water adventure.

23 19 Castle Street

The birthplace of broadcasting in Wales

In the closing years of the 19th century, Guglielmo Marconi developed long-range wireless technology that enabled signals to be transmitted over land and sea. Several private enterprises started to make household radio sets, but until there were broadcasts, there was no need for the public to buy them. These manufacturers collaborated to create the British Broadcasting Company to generate demand for their product.

In 1922, the first BBC broadcast was made in England, and in February the following year, it was Wales' turn. By the time of that first Welsh broadcast, 200 early adopters had bought a licence to listen. A studio was set up in a room above the music shop at 19 Castle Street. Minutes before the broadcast was due to begin, technicians were still stringing wires across the ceiling, but they managed to start the programme at the allotted time – 5pm on 13 February, 1923 – by the skin of their teeth.

Mostyn Thomas had the honour of singing the first ever Welsh-language song on radio at 9.30pm the same evening. He was nervous, as microphones were also a new technology and hard to use, and he had little time to practise. However, the Welsh folk song 'Dafydd y Garreg Wen' rang out across the airwaves at the allotted time, to the delight of his Welsh-speaking audience.

Those in Bristol listening to the same radio station were not as thrilled about the use of the Welsh language, which resulted in the station splitting into two. This set the precedent for Wales having its own broadcasts, ultimately opening the door for BBC Wales, S4C and Radio Cymru. Broadcasting in this way was a highly successful marketing strategy, as 300,000 radio licences were bought in 1936, which suggests a similar number of households had radio sets. By this point, the BBC had morphed into the British Broadcasting Corporation, a state broadcaster with a Royal Charter.

Address 17–19 Castle Street, Cardiff, CF10 1BS | Getting there Bus 44, 45, 49 or 50 to Castle Street; train to Cardiff Central | Hours Viewable from the outside only | Tip The studio might not have been very attractive, but the view from the window certainly was! The statues on the castle's clock tower are 3m tall and represent planets in the solar system. Tours of the tower are run over the summer months (www.cardiffcastle.com/castle-tours).

24 Cathays Heritage Library

A butterfly for books

On approaching Cathays Library, it is clear that this is not a standard municipal library. Two large stone-built halls with tall windows and high roofs, reminiscent of the engine houses of a water-treatment works, form butterfly wings. These are joined to each other by a lower, single-storey entrance hall, topped with a spire. It is one of the first Arts and Crafts buildings in Wales with a butterfly plan, which perfectly suits its corner site. The result is an entrance in a welcoming embrace of stone.

Inside, the rich tones of a polished wooden reception desk greet visitors, overlit with a domed stained glass window and surrounded by wooden parquet flooring. When the library was built in 1906, one wing was for adult readers and one for children. A separate ladies' reading room suggests that women were not considered to be either!

Cardiff has Andrew Carnegie to thank for this beautiful library. As a teenager, his family emigrated from Scotland to the United States to escape economic hardship, and the American Dream came true for him. He invested in the machinery of the Industrial Revolution – railway carriages, blast furnaces, iron mills and oil refining equipment – and founded a steelworks. In 1901, he sold the business for a cool $480 million and decided to spend some of his fortune on philanthropic deeds, such as donating funds to build libraries.

The building now provides access to the regular range of library books. However, its speciality is the history of Cardiff. If you want to find out more about your family, your street or the development of the city, this is the place to go. Apart from the reception desk and flooring, this is a thoroughly modern library with roller shelves full of interesting documents including leaflets, maps, street directories, parish registers, photographs and periodicals. Much of the data has been scanned onto microfilm, and there is, of course, access to extensive online resources – and real people, willing and able to help you with your search.

Address Fairoak Road, Cardiff, CF24 4PW, +44 (0) 292 078 5580, www.cardiffhubs.co.uk | **Getting there** Several buses to Library/Gladstone School; train to Cathays (16-minute walk) | **Hours** Mon, Wed & Sat 9am–5pm, Tue & Thu 10am–6pm | **Tip** Whitchurch and Canton libraries, both impressive buildings, were also built with endowments from Andrew Carnegie.

25 Celebration of Life Garden

If you go down to the park today…

If you suffer from arkoudaphobia (a fear of bears), the Celebration of Life Garden is certainly to be avoided, although all the bears here are friendly. A small bear holds a 'welcome' sign, large bears carved from wood stand sentinel on the grass, and from above, you can see that the whole park is shaped like a bear. The paths form the body, and the seating area is its head, with a curved bench for a smile, a sculpture for a nose and more benches for the eyes. For most, of course, teddy bears are comforting; a friend when they need one, always available for a *cwtsh*.

And that's what this park is for, too. It's close to Noah's Ark Children's Hospital. Just a short walk from the smell of antiseptic and fear of an uncertain future, patients and their families can spend time outside, playing with the bears or enjoying a teddy bears' picnic. In spring, daffodils provide some cheer before the surrounding trees burst into leaf. Time spent outdoors in nature reduces stress and improves recovery times, so this park is a godsend.

People go to the garden to play, to regroup and to mourn. Sometimes it is quiet. At others, it is full of riotous life. The Dreams & Wishes charity helps to create unforgettable memories for seriously ill children and their families. Whether it's a ride in a supercar, a trip to London or a full police escort for the drive to the prom, the experiences they organise give families something to look forward to and a happy time to remember. The charity created this garden to support families and children on a regular basis, too, when they are visiting the hospital.

This bear-shaped oasis reminds us all that, even in the face of illness and uncertainty, there is still room for wonder, play and connection. Many visitors leave with a renewed strength and resilience as well as memories, ready to face whatever challenges lie ahead.

Address Heath Park, King George V Drive East, Cardiff, CF14 4AY, www.outdoorcardiff.com/parks | Getting there Train to Heath Low Level (15-minute walk); several buses to Heath Hospital's main entrance | Hours Accessible 24 hours | Tip Head a little further into Heath Park to get refreshments from Brodies Coffee Co takeaway counter.

26 A Century of Topiary

From poison to pageantry

Since topiary was first introduced to Europe by the Romans, its fashionability has waxed and waned, although not in a 'fast fashion' sense. The first revival lasted for a couple of centuries, and the second has been in play for a century and a half to date.

Alexandra Park in Penarth was created in 1901–02 and named after the new King Edward VII's wife, Queen Alexandra. In 1913, 48 yew trees were planted. A few years after World War II, the cenotaph was added to commemorate the dead, the garden of remembrance was opened, and the council started to clip the yews into ornamental shapes. When the first trees were clipped, did they have any idea of what they had started? Despite changes in horticultural fashion and budget challenges, the yews of Alexandra Park are still being clipped today, creating an impressive display.

Yew trees are ideal for topiary as they grow bushy when cut back, live for a long time and have year-round, deep green foliage. Clipped well, they create tidy topiary that can be geometric, freeform, or cut to resemble animals, such as the birds that flank the path from Rectory Road. The trees are particularly impressive in the winter months when little else is in leaf, or frost highlights their forms.

Although highly useful in many ways, yew trees do have a downside. Almost every part of the tree is toxic to humans – it is a good idea to wear gloves when handling yew and a mask when cutting or sanding it. Ironically, this toxicity is part of what makes yew valuable in medicine, as the poisonous compounds can also be harnessed to fight cancer cells. For a while, clippings from parks like this were bought by the makers of Tamoxifen, a chemotherapy drug used to treat cancer. However, there are more efficient ways of making the treatment now, such as semi-synthetic production and cultivating yew trees for that purpose.

Address Alexandra Park, Rectory Road, Penarth, Cardiff, CF64 3AN, www.valeofglamorgan.gov.uk/en/enjoying/parks-and-gardens | **Getting there** Train to Penarth; several buses to Rectory Road or Penarth Pier | **Hours** Daily 8am–dusk | **Tip** To the east of the bandstand (downhill), the park also has a small children's playground.

27 Chance & Counters

Tabletop treasures

For a while, it seemed as though computer games would finish off the board game industry. However, that has not been the case. For the last few years, the board game industry has seen steady growth, driven by the need for social interaction in an increasingly technology-dominated society. Board games are entertaining, intellectually stimulating and designed to provide endorphin boosts, which is why they are so popular. In achieving this, they also improve cognitive function and strengthen social bonds.

Monopoly, Scrabble and chess continue to dominate the market, at least in part because so many are familiar with the format, enabling play with a wide range of others. However, the rise in popularity of board game cafés gives you an opportunity to introduce yourself to a wider range of games. In a board game café, you can eat, drink, laugh, build worlds, slay dragons, cooperate with your friends or compete for glory. Some games focus on storytelling and role-playing, while others challenge players with resource management or diplomatic negotiation.

In Chance & Counters, you can choose from over 650 games. If you don't know which to plump for, just ask the knowledgeable staff, who act as curators. They will help you to decide which is the most appropriate game for you and your group, considering the amount of time you have available. They will even give you a quick rundown of the rules to set you off in the right direction.

Board games are very popular in the UK, and continue to experience a steady rise in interest. You are therefore bound to find some friends who would love to join you for a fun night out. Chance & Counters also runs a weekly social evening when you have an opportunity to meet and play games with people outside your existing social circle. For larger groups, Chance & Counters has a separate room that can be privately booked.

Address First floor, 23 High Street, Cardiff, CF10 1PT, www.chanceandcounters.com/cardiff | Getting there Bus 44, 45, 49 or 50 to Castle Street; train to Cardiff Central. Look for the sandwich board on the pavement and yellow railings across the door. | Hours Mon & Tue 5–11pm, Wed & Thu noon–11pm, Fri & Sat noon–midnight, Sun noon–9pm | Tip If you like playing war games, then you might be tempted by the Warhammer shop a few doors down at 20 High Street.

28 Charter for Trees, Woods and People

Democracy takes root

The democratisation of Britain started with the Magna Carter and then the Charter of the Forest, and 800 years on, a new charter has led to communities committing to the health of contemporary forests and trees.

Medieval forests were areas of land that the king had claimed for his personal use to raise and hunt deer, and there were punitive punishments for those who broke 'forest law'. These forests were areas that commoners had previously been able to use for resources, and many were plunged into desperate circumstances by the designation. This was no minor issue – at one point, as much as 30 per cent of England was designated 'forest'.

The Charter of the Forest was initially part of the Magna Carta but was separated in 1217. It aimed to clarify the rights and privileges associated with the royal forests. As part of the democratisation process, more power was given to noblemen, who had land returned to them that had been unlawfully taken by previous monarchs as forest. They were now permitted to hunt on their own land, which led to the creation of many 'deer parks'. And the punishments for breaking forest law were relaxed – for killing the king's deer, you might now face a fine or imprisonment instead of death or mutilation.

Over time, democratisation has spread across the population, and the Charter for Trees, Woods and People reflects what is important to ordinary people about woods and trees. The 10 principles in the charter were based on 60,000 stories about what people value about their woods and trees. Now there are over 600 community groups, known as 'Charter Branches', who have signed their community up to these principles.

When the new charter was signed, an oak pole was carved for each of the 10 principles. This is the only one that made it to Wales, illustrating the importance of 'celebrating the power of trees to inspire'.

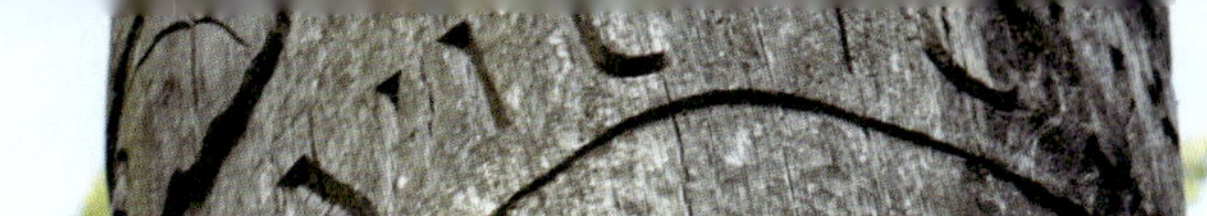

Address Bute Park, Cardiff, CF10 3RB, www.bute-park.com | **Getting there** Several buses to Cardiff Bridge; train to Cardiff Central | **Hours** Daily 7.30am–dusk | **Tip** The charter pole is in Bute Park, an ideal place for a stroll and a picnic.

29 Chinese Cemetery

A peaceful place to rest

Cardiff has long been a racially diverse city, as the coal boom brought workers from around the world. However, that does not mean that the relationship between different parties has always been easy.

Around the turn of the 20th century, it was far cheaper to employ someone to work on your ship from one of China's treaty ports than a British one. Therefore, a lot of ships had Chinese sailors on board. Inevitably, some of these sailors settled ashore, providing services to their countrymen, such as accommodation, food supply and laundries. As with many immigrants and expatriates, Chinese communities tended to stick together because of their shared cultural heritage and the language challenges associated with living in a new country.

When things get tough, it is easy to blame immigrants for all sorts of ills, from losing your job to 'stealing' local women. And this is what happened in South Wales in the early 1900s. Rising prices and falling wages led to the Great Unrest, and in one of the riots in 1911, every single Chinese laundry in Cardiff was attacked.

Another wave of Chinese immigrants arrived in Cardiff a few decades later when land reform in Hong Kong drove agricultural workers to Britain looking for a better life. Around 4,000 people of Chinese descent now live in Cardiff, most of whom are part of the second or third generation living in the city. In Chinese culture, as in so many others, burial rituals are important. Having a dedicated section of the cemetery allows Chinese community members to meet their cultural obligations without having to ship bodies back to China.

These days, you won't find many Chinese laundries in Cardiff. In fact, you won't find many laundries at all. What you will find are plenty of Chinese restaurants in which to eat, as the advent of the electric washing machine led to laundries being closed down and converted into restaurants.

Address Pantmawr Cemetery, Pantmawr Road, Cardiff, CF14 7TD, www.cardiffbereavement.co.uk/cemeteries | Getting there Bus 21 to Caer Wenallt South | Hours Daily 9.30am–4.15pm | Tip Every Chinese New Year, which falls in January or February, there is a celebration at Cardiff Central Library Hub.

30_Chip Alley

Cardiff's late-night-feast street

If you ever have the munchies after a night out in Cardiff, you'll find what you need on Caroline Street. But ask a local where Caroline Street is, and you might receive a blank look – to locals, it's known as 'Chip Alley', 'Chippy Lane' or 'Chippy Street'.

What started life as a typical city street with a range of shops, including a watchmaker, cobbler, draper, jeweller, hairdresser, grocer and butcher, has gradually transformed into a late-night food hub as chip shops and takeaways opened to cater to the post-pub and club crowd. In the 1970s and '80s, it was run down and close to derelict. In the early 2000s, the brewery on one side of the street moved out and was transformed into the Brewery Quarter, increasing the number of people in the area with late-night munchies. Caroline Street was pedestrianised, and over time it became the go-to spot for anyone craving a bite after dark.

If you want smashed avocado on organic sourdough for breakfast, Chip Alley is probably not the place for you. On the other hand, if you're after some flavour-rich and nutrient-poor fast food to round off a night out, then this is the place to go, whether it's a kebab, curry or fish and chips (with or without curry sauce) that you're craving.

Chip Alley isn't just about food – it's a Cardiff institution. This is where students gather after a night out to share a portion of chips, where sports fans relive the match over a battered sausage, and even where theatregoers head for a quick bite on the way home. It's as much a part of Cardiff's culture as the castle or the Principality Stadium.

So, next time you're on a big night out that's lasted into the early hours, follow your nose to Chip Alley and experience a Cardiff tradition. Just watch out for all those takeaway wrappers scattered across the street, ready to provide some banana-skin moments as they slide away under your weary feet.

Address Caroline Street, Cardiff, CF10 1FF | Getting there Train to Cardiff Central; several buses to Wyndham Arcade | Hours Street accessible 24 hours; serving times vary, but generally cover 10am–4am | Tip For more upmarket food, head towards the castle to High Street and Church Street, where there are several good restaurants.

31 Clive Road Ghost Sign

Bread of Heaven

The property at 135 Clive Road was once the home of a Dibble's bakery, whose loaves won plaudits, including silver and bronze medals at the 1913 London Baker's Exhibition. This sign advertises that Dibble's was licensed to make Turog loaves. In the early 20th century, Turog bread was touted as a healthy alternative to white bread that was lighter and longer lasting than other brown breads. The millers created what they claimed to be an exclusive process that made Turog loaves perfectly digestible while maintaining all the health benefits of the wheat. This process involved partially cooking the wheat as it was ground. The resulting flour apparently made a light, crusty loaf that cut without crumbling and stayed fresh for days. The millers were so confident that the public would love the 'deliciously nutty' flavour, they offered to send applicants a trial loaf.

Since then, the baking industry has changed significantly. The Chorleywood method of bread production was developed in the 1960s. This enabled bakers to produce a loaf from flour to baked, sliced and wrapped in a much shorter timescale, using wheat flour from the UK, which was often lower in protein and therefore did not make such good bread using the traditional method. This bread-making process, which adds fats, additional yeast and chemicals as well as using high-speed mixing, drove the expansion of industrial bread production and the decline of local bakeries.

In recent years, artisan breads and those made using traditional methods have grown in popularity, but a significant proportion of bread consumed in the UK and a growing number of countries worldwide is made using the Chorleywood method. The health benefits of bread that has been slowly fermented are now becoming better understood, so the pendulum may start to swing back in favour of smaller, more local bakeries, like the one that once operated here on Clive Road.

Address 135 Clive Road, Cardiff, CF5 1GN | Getting there Bus 61, 604 or 606 to Clive Road or Fern Street, or bus 25, 62 or 63 to Dulwich House; train to Waun-Gron Park (21-minute walk) | Hours Viewable from the outside only | Tip If you love freshly baked bread, there are several bakeries to choose from in nearby Canton, including Brutons at 224 Cowbridge Road East (www.brutonsthebakers.co.uk).

32 Cornerstone

From ballast to buildings

Cargo ships are expensive to buy, maintain and run. Whether or not a vessel contains cargo, it needs fuel and a crew to sail it, both of which cost money. This makes an empty one more of a liability than an asset. If you owned a shipping company, you would want to run your ships full of cargo at all times to offset those costs. However, this is not always possible. When Cardiff was exporting at a rate of two million tonnes of goods a year, imports were at a much lower level. This imbalance inevitably meant that some ships arrived in the port empty.

Empty cargo ships are not just a financial drain. Ships are designed to carry weight. When empty, they are top heavy and unstable, liable to take on water, capsize and sink. One way yachts deal with this is to have a weighted keel below the hull, counterbalancing the weight above. However, for a large ship, that is impractical, as the keel would be enormous and it would be unable to enter docks. Another solution is to carry low-value heavy materials at the bottom of the hold and unload them before filling up with the new cargo. This is not an ideal solution – it is expensive and time consuming to load and unload, and the receiving port will have ever-increasing piles of ballast to dispose of. This situation can be partially mitigated if a use can be found for that ballast. Cue the building boom that was taking place in Cardiff at the same time as the growth in trade.

The church that is now known as Cornerstone was the first in Cardiff to be built in the neo-Gothic style, so it is an important part of the city's architectural history. If you look at the walls, you can see that it was also faced with numerous different types of rock. This was the ballast taken from a ship that was to be filled with coal before returning to the Middle East. The church is therefore also an important part of the city's shipping history.

Address Charles Street, Cardiff, CF10 2GA, +44 (0) 292 049 4425, www.cornerstonecardiff.org, cornerstone@spiros.co.uk | Getting there Several buses to Churchill Way; train to Cardiff Queen Street or Cardiff Central | Hours Mon–Sat 10am–5pm, Sun 9am–4pm | Tip Cardiff Cathedral (Roman Catholic) is opposite Cornerstone. Destroyed during World War II, it was rebuilt in the 1950s (www.cardiffcathedral.org.uk).

33 Corp Market

The cross that turned full circle

During Cardiff's booming years as a coal port, the town's population grew exponentially, as did the need for accommodation for visitors. Cardiff Corporation saw the need (or possibly the financial opportunity) and built a commercial hotel on land at Canton Cross, previously Canton Market.

The Corporation was successfully leased out by the council for over a century. Less than a mile from Cardiff City Stadium, it became a favourite hangout for Bluebirds fans on matchdays. But in 2016, the brewery decided not to renew the lease, and the council decided it would be a good time to sell. Four years later, when the COVID pandemic hit, it had been sold but remained empty.

During a period when people could only meet with others outdoors, the car park behind the pub presented another opportunity to serve the community – this time, with pop-up street food. The Corporation Yard proved to be popular, so when local people were once again allowed to mingle indoors, it extended into the building.

This building at Canton Cross has now turned full circle, from market to market, while retaining its core as a meeting place. The imposing brown brick and white exterior opens into an airy interior that successfully blends industrial chic with warmth and homeliness. The diverse range of offerings reflects Cardiff's vibrant culture and community spirit. Local artisans share space with independent retailers, and the layout encourages exploration, not knowing what treasure you might find around the next turn. A central bar and café serves as the heart of the space, offering somewhere for friends to meet, families to gather and solo visitors to feel part of the community. Whether you are into role-playing games or Italian food, books or knitting, houseplants or mental health – or simply want a cup of tea, a pint of beer or a haircut – there's something for you at Corp Market.

Address 188 Cowbridge Road East, Cardiff, CF5 1GW, www.facebook.com/CorpMarket | **Getting there** Bus 66 to Market Place or Grey Lane, several to Canton Library; train to Cardiff Central (30-minute walk) | **Hours** Tue–Sat 10am–5pm, bar and coffee shop 10am–11pm | **Tip** If you like the food offerings at Corp Market, check out Snails Deli in Rhiwbina, which sells homemade and local food in the café and shop (www.snailsdeli.com).

34 Cromwell's Stone

Civil War slaughter

The story of the British Civil Wars in the Cardiff area is one of fickle allegiances and great loss. Initially, most of the gentry in South Wales put aside their differences and supported the king, offering men to the Royalist armies. Of course, the men themselves had no say in the matter and were used as cannon fodder, dying in great numbers.

After significant losses in the first three years of the war, the local lords were beginning to wonder whether they had backed the wrong side. King Charles I visited Cardiff in person and stayed at the castle for a week, trying to gain ongoing support and men from South Wales. However, he was unsuccessful, and the local lords switched sides, installing a Parliamentarian as the Governor of Cardiff Castle. The Royalists attacked but were quickly repelled and driven out of the area.

The first Civil War finished with Charles' defeat and imprisonment in 1646, but he was not a quitter, and continued to negotiate while officially incarcerated. He realised that by supporting Presbyterians, he could generate some powerful allegiances. This led to Major-General Laugharne switching sides and becoming a Royalist once again, with some of his influential friends in tow. They amassed an army of mainly untrained farmers and headed towards Cardiff for the Royalist cause.

Oliver Cromwell got wind of their plans and dashed to the area with his highly trained and battle-hardened New Model Army. The battle at St Fagan's was short but deadly, with the Parliamentarians victorious and the Royalists retreating beyond Cowbridge.

During the Civil Wars, the Parliamentarians ransacked Llandaff Cathedral, destroying or removing many of the church's treasures, and used the building as a stable and tavern. It is said that Cromwell tied his horse to this stone in the centre of the village during his stay in the area.

Address Outside the Maltsters Arms Hotel, Cardiff Road, Llandaff, Cardiff, CF5 2DF | **Getting there** Bus 25, 62, 63, 122 or 124 to Black Lion; train to Waun-Gron Park (17-minute walk) | **Hours** Accessible 24 hours | **Tip** If you fancy some horse riding yourself, Cardiff Riding School is nearby in Pontcanna Fields (www.outdoorcardiff.com/cardiff-riding-school).

35 Dead Canary

Speakeasy style

As you might imagine from the name, the Dead Canary is not your usual cocktail bar, and the cocktails they sell are not your usual cocktails. At the time of writing, each drink is linked to a dark Welsh legend, with the story told and illustrated on the menu. The cocktails, themes and stories sometimes change, but the overall concept remains the same.

Will you spend the evening with the Hag of the Mist, wondering what her siren call sounds like, while hoping never to hear it, as it leads unsuspecting souls to their deaths? Or would you rather swim with the Swan Maiden, who had her wings and beak stolen so she could be kept in captivity? The cheerful golden petals of Rhossili Sunflowers might seem like a more upbeat cocktail – until you read the story of the *Helvetia* shipwreck, the skeleton of which protrudes from the sands of the bay nearby.

Whichever cocktail you choose, your first challenge is to find the entrance to the Dead Canary. It does not sport a large sign, lit with neon. It does not even sport a window. And it is not at the front of the building. Once you have reserved your table, the staff will tell you how to find the door. Even when you get there, you might not be entirely convinced that you have reached the right place, unless you spot a clue: perhaps a birdcage hanging above the door or a small gold feather painted on the wall.

If you have chosen the right door and pressed the right bell, you will soon be ushered into the building and shown to your table. The staff are attentive and knowledgeable, happy to spend time with customers to talk through the options and help you choose. With staff as creative and familiar with cocktails as they have in the Dead Canary, it is, of course, possible to order from a long list of everyday options as well as their own menu, but why would you do that when you can benefit from the full flourish of their genius instead?

Address Barrack Lane, Cardiff, CF10 2FR, +44 (0) 7874 928366, www.thedeadcanary.co.uk | Getting there Several buses to Churchill Way; train to Cardiff Queen Street or Cardiff Central | Hours Tue–Sun 5pm–late | Tip If you prefer living birds, there are good birdwatching opportunities at Lisvane & Llanishen Reservoirs, including a hide (www.lisvane-llanishen.com).

36 Dead Man's Alley

The churchyard shortcut

For three centuries, Cardiff Gaol stood next to St John the Baptist Church in the centre of Cardiff. In those days, some prisoners were publicly executed at the gaol as well as being imprisoned there, so perhaps it was handy having the churchyard next door. Capital punishment is, of course, illegal in the UK now, but the last execution took place as recently as 1964, and in the 19th century, 20 people were hanged at Cardiff Gaol. By the middle of the century, the gaol was seriously overcrowded, so another, larger prison was built, and this one was demolished.

When a market hall was built on the site of the old gaol, it was a little less handy having a graveyard next door, as shoppers had to walk all around the outside edge to reach the entrance. So, the council made a deal with the church. People would be allowed to walk across the middle of the churchyard to the market hall, and in exchange, the council would maintain the already-full section of the churchyard on the far side of the path. To this day, it is looked after by the council, and open to the public as St John's Garden.

The path itself is not a public right of way, and the tradition of closing it on Good Friday has been retained as a reminder that this is the case. Looking closely at the ground as you walk towards the market, you might notice several metal numbers embedded in the path. The original numbers were made from brass and wore over time, so the brass was replaced with stainless steel when the path was re-laid. Have you ever wondered what the numbers mean? They mark the position of several family vaults that lie, or used to lie, under the path. No one seems to know whether the vaults were moved when the path was laid or whether visitors to the market are walking over ancient graves. Either way, this is the reason for the path's nickname of 'Dead Man's Alley'.

Address St John Street, Cardiff, CF10 1GJ | Getting there Bus 44, 45, 49 or 50 to Castle Street; train to Cardiff Central | Hours Accessible 24 hours | Tip For those curious about the dead who do not depart, Dark Wales Tours offer ghost tours of St Fagan's and Insole Court, as well as other places in Wales (www.darkwalestours.co.uk).

37 Death Junction

Hanged on hearsay

It seems that peddling and falling for fakc news is not reserved for the 21st century. In the 1670s, Titus Oates faked his conversion to Catholicism to join Jesuit seminaries overseas. On his return to England, he swore that English Catholics were plotting to kill the king and start a religious uprising, intending to slaughter Protestants. It seems that his statement was not fact checked, and the 'Popish Plot' was believed by many, including the House of Commons. This resulted in a religious witch hunt in 1678–79. Catholics were tried on trumped-up charges, and several were executed, including two from Cardiff.

Philip Evans was born in Wales and moved to Flanders to study at the English college in Saint Omer. There, he joined the Jesuits and was ordained in 1675. His first mission involved a return to South Wales, where he served for four years. As a result of the Popish Plot, a large bounty was placed on his head. The local police offered him a chance to convert to Protestantism, pledge allegiance to the king and accept the king's supremacy in all religious matters. He refused and consequently was arrested and incarcerated in the castle.

For three weeks, he was in solitary confinement before being moved to join Father John Lloyd in his cell. It took five months before either man could be taken to court, as no one was prepared to testify that they were priests.

Eventually, someone did, and the two men were hung, drawn and quartered at what is now the junction of five roads. Philip Evans was the first to die, and his parting words were, 'I die for God and religion's sake'. John Lloyd had to watch his excruciating death, knowing that the same was in store for him. Nevertheless, his parting words were, 'I die in the true Catholic and apostolic faith... with those three virtues: faith, hope and charity'. It seems that they died with dignity.

Address 227 City Road, Cardiff, CF24 3JD | Getting there Several buses to Inverness Place or Strathnairn Street; train to Cathays (15-minute walk); on-street parking nearby | Hours Accessible 24 hours | Tip Catholics were not the only ones in Cardiff to be persecuted. Rawlins White was a Protestant who paid for his life at the hands of the Catholic authorities. He has a memorial on St Mary Street.

38 Dinas Powis Hillfort

An internationally important post-Roman site

When you see a hillfort in the UK, it is easy to assume that it dates back to the Iron Age, as so many do. However, Dinas Powis is a little different. There is evidence that there was an earlier settlement here in the late Stone Age and early Bronze Age. Although difficult to see as a whole because of the forest that now covers the hill, there are four sets of banks and ditches protecting the site. The first of these is thought to have been constructed during the late Bronze Age or early Iron Age, when the site was still occupied. People stayed here for long enough to move from being hunter-gatherers to farmers, with agricultural land developed within the earthworks south of the fort.

By the early Roman period, the site was abandoned, but after Roman rule ended in the 5th century, an elite family occupied the fort. It is the quality and quantity of finds from the following 200 years that makes this site internationally important. Those who lived here had pottery that was imported from the Mediterranean and southern France, and Frankish glass from the area around the Rhine. They also used metals and produced ornamental metalwork. Some similar finds have been found in Tintagel Castle, suggesting a trading link, or at the very least, that this site was of equally high status. During this period, it is thought that the remaining three sets of banks and ditches were constructed, suggesting the need for a greater degree of protection.

At some point in the 7th or 8th century, the site was abandoned. This is likely to be when trees started to recolonise the promontory. We know for sure that this is an ancient woodland, which means there has been tree cover here for at least 400 years, and possibly longer. The hillfort and surrounding woodlands are now open-access land with paths enabling exploration. From these paths, the extent of the protective ringworks becomes evident.

Address Dinas Powys, Cardiff, CF64 | Getting there Park on Highwalls Avenue, Dinas Powys, CF64 4AQ; bus 305 to Dinas Powys Square; train to Dinas Powys (15-minute walk to Highwalls Avenue). From Highwalls Avenue, take the footpath east across the golf course then downhill. Turn left at the bottom of the valley. At the information board, follow the path uphill onto the hillfort. | Hours Accessible 24 hours | Tip The Star Inn in Dinas Powys is a popular place to dine out.

39_FabLab Cardiff

Where imagination meets innovation

Things are moving fast in the world of technology-supported manufacturing. 3D printers can now create things from rigid and flexible plastics, biodegradable materials, ceramics and powdered metal, sometimes using more than one material at once. This is opening the door for significant advances in manufacturing across many sectors. Large-scale printing is being developed in the construction industry and for complex parts such as aeroplane wings. On a smaller scale, prosthetics and other medical accoutrements can be tailored to the recipient, improving quality of life.

As this technology develops, it promises to revolutionise manufacturing, enabling individual items to be made where they are needed, when they are needed. This should significantly reduce waste by reducing the need to hold stock. Food is already being printed, which could dramatically reduce carbon emissions, and research into bioprinting organs could make organ waiting lists a thing of the past and save thousands of lives.

At FabLab Cardiff, you can use any of their machines to try 3D printing and other technologically advanced machinery, such as a flatbed CNC machine and laser cutters. FabLab can help with materials and provide training to develop the skills needed to make the most of this facility, whether for one person or a whole team. A local chocolatier makes moulds for bespoke chocolates, and a classic-car restorer makes parts he can no longer source. One local woman who had had a mastectomy made herself a false boob that exactly matches her other one.

The team at the lab is there to support local businesses, artists and others in bringing ideas to fruition. If you're unsure whether something is possible, call them. How could your business or school make the most of these advances? This is where you can try before committing and have fun playing with your ideas.

Address Cardiff Metropolitan University, Llandaff Campus, 200 Western Avenue, Cardiff, CF5 2YB, +44 (0) 292 020 5572, www.fablabcardiff.com, fablab@cardiffmet.ac.uk | **Getting there** Bus M1 or 1 or 2 City Circle to Cardiff Met Llandaff (outside); train to Waun-Gron Park (30-minute walk) | **Hours** Mon–Thu 10am–5pm, Fri 10am–2pm | **Tip** If you feel the need for some fresh air after all that creativity, head 150 metres north to the river, where there are paths on both sides in both directions.

40 Flat Holm Radio

The birth of wireless

Gugliemo Marconi was a young man who loved a challenge. When he started to work on long-range wireless communication, other people had already been trying to crack it for 50 years. Some might have thought it impossible, but he was determined to make it happen. While living in Italy, he successfully transmitted signals for over a mile, but the Italian authorities did not see the potential benefits of this technology and, therefore, did not support his work. Frustrated, Marconi found a supporter in William Preece, the Engineer-in-Chief at the British Post Office, and moved to London at the age of 21 to pursue his dreams.

It did not take him long to successfully transmit signals across London. When he wanted to do the same over the sea, he found an ally in George Kemp, a Post Office engineer in Cardiff. In May 1897, they erected one mast on Laverock Point just south of Penarth, and another on Flat Holm Island, a few miles away in the Bristol Channel.

On 11 May, the first signal was sent. It failed to arrive. Throughout that day and the next, the experiment was unsuccessful. Again, some might have been discouraged, but Marconi persisted. It was on the third day, 13 May, that the tests succeeded. After continuing for a few days in different meteorological conditions, the team increased their ambition and moved the receiving mast to Brean Down Fort near Weston-Super-Mare on the far side of the Bristol Channel. It worked, and it was only a few years later that Marconi successfully set up the first radio link across the Atlantic Ocean.

This oversized hardwood sculpture of a radio was erected on the barrage to commemorate the development of wireless communication. Marconi is not mentioned on the sculpture thanks to an unsavoury aspect of his life linked with fascism and Nazism. This sculpture is designed to celebrate his work rather than his name.

Address Cardiff Barrage, Cardiff, CF10 4GA | Getting there Bus 305 to Barrage | Hours Accessible 24 hours | Tip There is a bronze plaque commemorating the first successful over-water radio transmission in St Lawrence churchyard in Lavernock.

41 Fred Keenor Statue

Pitch perfect

Wales is rightly proud of its sporting heritage, and rugby is often considered the country's national sport. But where does that leave football? A survey conducted by Nielsen in 2022 indicated that football is now the most popular sport in Wales based on the number of supporters and players.

And Cardiff's Fred Keenor was a giant of the sport. Born in 1894, he started to play for Cardiff City in 1912. Not long into his career, World War I disrupted play. Instead of fighting to win a game on a football pitch, he fought for King and Country – and his life, after being injured during the Battle of the Somme. Following a lengthy period of rehabilitation back in the UK, he was not sent back to the front line. Instead, he worked as a physical training instructor. Despite fears that his injury would stop him from ever playing at the top of his game again, he returned to Cardiff City once the war was over and was part of a highly successful team. In 1925, they reached the final of the FA Cup. They lost, but in 1927, they played again. This time, they won. This was quite an achievement – Cardiff City remains the only club outside England to have won the cup.

In 1921, the Football Association banned women from playing football. It was not until the 1970s that the ban was lifted, but women's football was always seen as inferior, not receiving the same funding or support as men's football. However, this changed in 2023, when players in the Welsh women's team started to receive the same pay as players in the Welsh men's team. Maybe one day, one of the pioneering female players will also be considered enough of a sporting giant to have her statue alongside Fred Keenor's in front of the national stadium. After all, Jess Fishlock was the first Welsh player, male or female, to earn 100 caps for her country. That's certainly an achievement worth celebrating!

Address Cardiff City Stadium, Leckwith Road, Cardiff, CF11 8AZ | Getting there Several buses to Hadfield Road or Jubilee Park; train to Ninian Park; on-site parking | Hours Accessible 24 hours | Tip For a friendly kick-around, Jubilee Recreation Ground is immediately to the north of the stadium.

42 Gift of Life Stone

A different kind of hero

Cardiff's Alexandra Gardens sport the Welsh National War Memorial to those lost in the two world wars, and a series of smaller memorial stones placed around the park. These commemorate a variety of people, including those of diverse ethnic and commonwealth heritage who have fought for this country, those who fought in the Falklands, and even those who fought in the Spanish Civil War. As well as the usual war-related memorials, there are others, including one for everyone affected by the thalidomide tragedy, and this one for all organ and tissue donors.

In the UK, over 4,000 people receive donated organs and tissues every year, including around 1,000 kidneys from living donors. A report in 2008 identified several bottlenecks in the organ donation process and made 14 recommendations for improvement. This has led to a 95% increase in deceased donors and a reduction of 20 per cent in the waiting lists. However, there are still several thousand people waiting for an organ.

Now that there is assumed consent across the UK (rather than the old system of having to opt in), more organs are offered for donation. However, grieving families unsure of their loved one's wishes can still stop it from happening, so it is essential that everyone makes their wishes known.

Several of our organs can be donated, including the heart, lungs, kidneys, liver, pancreas and small bowel. Possible tissue donations include skin, bone, heart valves and corneas. This means that one donor can give the gift of life to several people on the waiting list, and the gift of sight to two others. Now the number of donors has increased, the focus is on using new technologies and techniques so that a greater proportion of offered organs can be used, and each donor can save more lives. A further focus is being put on the inequalities in the system, to ensure that no sectors of society have to wait for longer than others.

Address Alexandra Gardens, Cardiff, CF10 3NQ, www.outdoorcardiff.com | **Getting there** Several buses to College Road; train to Cathays | **Hours** Accessible 24 hours | **Tip** The Cardiff 10K race sees thousands of runners pounding the streets and parks of Cardiff, many raising money for their favourite charity, including Kidney Wales who donated the Gift of Life Stone (www.cardiff10k.cymru).

43 Glamorganshire Canal

Birding paradise

The Glamorganshire Canal was built towards the end of the 18th century to bring iron from Merthyr Tydfil to the port at Cardiff. It was no mean feat; with a rise of 165 metres, 50 locks were required to defeat gravity. However, canal transportation promised to be faster and more efficient than using the roads, which were often nothing more than a track that might become a muddy quagmire in winter and bake into ruts in the summer.

An Act of Parliament for the canal was passed, and compulsory land purchase began. Four years later, all 25 miles of the canal were operational. The owner was a little too greedy, which led to a minor rebellion, and some tramroads were built to limit the distance the iron was transported on the water. However, there was no serious competition until the Taff Vale Railway opened in 1841. Even then, there was enough business to go around, and the canal remained profitable for another 35 years.

The first sign of trouble was in 1876 when the company could not pay the full eight per cent dividend allowed by the act. After that, profits continued to drop, and the canal started to fall into disrepair. The first part closed in 1898, and its final death knell sounded in 1951 when a dredger destroyed the bottom set of lock gates and emptied the last navigable section.

Most of the canal has now been filled in or built on. However, this delightful stretch remains on the outskirts of the city. Instead of being a hive of industrial activity, it is now a hive of wildlife activity. It is said to be one of the best places in the UK to spot kingfishers and the best birdwatching venue in Cardiff. This may be because of the range of habitats here, including old forest, scrub, flower meadows and, of course, wetlands. The canal sits in a country park that is easily accessed by public transport and many of the paths are wheelchair accessible, too.

Address Forest Farm Road, Cardiff, CF14 7JP, www.outdoorcardiff.com/parks | Getting there Train to Llandaff or Radyr; bus 25, 101 or 102 to Velindre Hospital | Hours Accessible 24 hours | Tip A short urban section of the Glamorganshire Canal has been recreated at the Queen Street end of Churchill Way in the city centre.

44_Gold Postbox

Geraint's golden monument

Conspicuous Royal Mail postboxes are familiar to us all, but they weren't always there. And they weren't always red. When the government first set up a postal monopoly, it introduced a standard fee for a letter to be delivered from one point to another in the UK. In towns, a 'bellman' walked around, ringing his bell and collecting mail to take to a receiving house (a precursor of a Post Office). However, for villagers, the receiving houses were often miles away, and the service remained challenging to access.

The author Anthony Trollope, who worked for the General Post Office at the time, noticed that some countries had resolved this issue by placing secure boxes in strategic places, into which people could post their letters. Before long, a trial was introduced on Jersey. It was deemed a success and introduced to the mainland in 1853.

The first boxes were painted red, but in 1859, the colour was standardised to green so the boxes were not too conspicuous. However, this proved unpopular as people struggled to find them. The colour was ultimately re-standardised, this time to 'pillar-box red'. Since then, all postboxes in the UK have been red, with only a handful of exceptions.

During a brief period in the 1930s, blue boxes were introduced for airmail letters. A handful of boxes were painted blue and emblazoned with THANK YOU NHS during the Coronavirus pandemic. And for the 2012 London Olympics, the Royal Mail honoured every UK athlete who won a gold medal. Each had a postbox painted gold in their hometown to commemorate their win, which is why there is now a very well-camouflaged postbox opposite the castle.

And why not celebrate the successes of the Cardiff-born Geraint Thomas, who was the first Welshman to win the Tour de France, as well as being a member of the pursuit cycling team that won in the London Olympics?

Address Castle Street, Cardiff, CF10 1BT | Getting there Bus 44, 45, 49 or 50 to Castle Street; train to Cardiff Central | Hours Accessible 24 hours | Tip To cycle around Cardiff yourself, you can hire bikes from one of Cardiff Pedal Power's two sites: one in Pontcanna and one on the bay (www.cardiffpedalpower.org).

45 Gorse

The first Michelin-starred restaurant in Cardiff

As the saying goes, 'When gorse is out of bloom, kissing is out of fashion'. These familiar spiky plants stud our landscape, and although they flower most profusely in summer, they do not stop over winter, brightening up even the dullest of days. Lean in close, and the flowers smell of coconut, perhaps one of the reasons they are so loved by pollinating insects.

To Tom Waters, chef and owner of Gorse, the plant reminds him of happy holidays at the Welsh seaside. Growing up in South Wales, he left to gain culinary experience elsewhere. His travels took him to several Michelin-starred restaurants around the UK, until the time was right to return home. He opened Gorse in May 2024 and earned Cardiff's first Michelin star in February the following year.

The intimate restaurant, with space for only 22 diners, is open to the kitchen, which means that customers are as likely to find themselves talking to the chefs as the front-of-house staff. The quality and provenance of the food served are paramount. Each dish is simple, letting that quality speak for itself, and prepared by a master chef who knows exactly which ingredients will work together.

Everything in the restaurant, from food to art to dinnerware, is sourced from Wales wherever possible, and no food is imported from overseas. The restaurant offers tasting menus likely to feature foods such as seaweeds, shellfish, and other Welsh delicacies. Crabs from Solva, wild mussels from St David's, salt-marsh lamb from the Gower and fallow deer from Breconshire have all featured on the menu, although it is subject to change depending on the season and availability. The vegetarian menu also has an array of mouthwatering dishes and ingredients, like hen of the woods, cultured laver butter and preserved roses. It seems that this Gorse is blooming, and unlikely to go out of fashion any time soon.

Address 186–188 King's Road, Pontcanna, Cardiff, CF11 9DF, +44 (0) 292 037 2055, www.gorserestaurant.co.uk, hello@gorserestaurant.co.uk | Getting there Bus 61 or 604 to Turberville Place or 25, 62 or 63 to Berthwin Street; train to Ninian Park (18-minute walk) | Hours See website for available reservations | Tip Home, in Penarth, also holds a Michelin star (www.homeatpenarth.co.uk).

46 Gorsedd Stones

A circle of culture

All traditions start somewhere, and the tradition of the Gorsedd rather incongruously started on Primrose Hill in London in 1792, rather than in Wales, as you might expect. Controversial historian Iolo Morganwg, who had a very active imagination, lived in London but wanted to celebrate his Welsh Celtic culture and heritage. He created a group called the Gorsedd of the Bards of the Isle of Britain (now Gorsedd Cymru), and they started to perform ceremonies based on pagan rites. Members of the Gorsedd are called druids, but they worship language and culture rather than gods.

In 1819, Morganwg decided to perform one of these ceremonies at the Carmarthenshire Eisteddfod. He created a circle of pebbles in the grounds of the Ivy Bush Hotel and spawned the pageantry that still characterises the National Eisteddfod two centuries later. The circle of pebbles became a circle of standing stones with a flat 'Logan Stone' in the middle. This provides a platform from which the Archdruid (head of the Gorsedd) can conduct the opening ceremony of the celebration.

And with ceremony comes regalia. The Archdruid wears golden robes. The robes of the main prize winners are white, those of artists and people who have passed an entry exam are green, and those of people who have been recognised for contributing to their community or Wales are blue.

The Eisteddfod is held in Welsh in the first week of August each year, swapping between communities in the north and south of the country. (Simultaneous interpretation to English is available.) In the past, each community that held an Eisteddfod was left with a stone circle, sometimes created from local rock and sometimes from rock representing different areas of Wales. These days, replica stones have replaced the real ones, but Cardiff retains Gorsedd stones from the 1978 Eisteddfod in Bute Park and the 1899 Eisteddfod in Gorsedd Gardens.

Address Bute Park, Cardiff, CF10 3RB, www.bute-park.com | **Getting there** Several buses to Cardiff Bridge; train to Cardiff Central | **Hours** Daily 7.30am–dusk | **Tip** There are several discovery trails in Bute Park. Head west from the Gorsedd stones to play on musical installations (www.bute-park.com/trails).

47 Greek Orthodox Church

A Byzantine beauty

With Greece's history of shipping, it is no surprise that the Greek ensign was often seen fluttering from ships as the port of Cardiff grew. Rather than simply arriving empty and leaving with coal, the Greek ships imported cereals to maximise income. Up to 200 entered Cardiff docks each year. As time went on and the port continued to thrive, some of the Greek sailors chose to settle in Cardiff, as did those from other nations.

When Greeks first started to worship in Cardiff, they did not have their own church. Instead, the congregation used the Norwegian church for their services. By the early years of the 20th century, there were enough Greeks in Cardiff to build their own place of worship. In 1906, the church was opened to great fanfare by a Greek diplomat from the consulate in Cardiff.

In the middle of the 20th century, two factors increased the Greek population in Cardiff. The first was World War II, when many Greek ships were not permitted to leave the port. The second was between 1955 and 1965, when Greece and Cyprus faced financial difficulties, and many Greeks had to find somewhere else to live.

Today, there are around 2,000 people in Saint Nicholas' community, as well as an influx of university students each year. A neighbouring building provides an alternative space for the community to congregate and celebrate outside the church.

The detailed mosaic over the church's entrance arch only hints at the richly decorated Byzantine-style church hidden behind. A fresco of Jesus looks down from the top of a dome, surrounded by other religious figures, all contrasting with a deep blue background. More portraits adorn the walls, this time with a golden background and framed in intricate wooden panels. Appropriately, the church is dedicated to Saint Nicholas. After all, he is the patron saint of sailors and merchants, among others, as this impressive mosaic illustrates so well.

Address Greek Church Street, Cardiff, CF10 5HA, +44 (0) 292 048 7889, www.stnikolaos.org.uk, stnicholascardiffgoc@gmail.com | **Getting there** Bus X2 or 304 to Callaghan Square; train to Cardiff Central | **Hours** Sun 11.45am–2.30pm for private prayer | **Tip** There are several Greek restaurants in Cardiff. The Hellenic Eatery in Cathays is a Welsh Restaurant Awards winner (www.thehelleniceatery.co.uk).

48 Gwyn Nicholls Memorial Gates

Play to your strengths

Gwyn Nicholls was a legend in Rugby Union at the turn of the 20th century. Known as the 'Prince of Threequarters', he earned 24 caps for Wales and captained 10 of those matches. The crowning moment of his career was captaining the 1905 team that beat the All Blacks.

Picture this: it's a foggy day, and Cardiff Arms Park is full of expectant supporters. The All Blacks have been romping their way across England, conceding few points, let alone matches. Everyone is expecting Wales to fall the same way. New Zealand's Haka has been unnerving their opponents. Could the Welsh counter the power of the Haka? Perhaps the Welsh could respond with their own superpower – their voices. Once the Haka has ended and the stadium is quiet, one lone voice is heard. Player Teddy Morgan has started to sing 'Land of My Fathers'. His voice is soon joined by those of the rest of the team. Then, magic happens. The crowd joins in. No one has ever heard anything like this at a sporting fixture before, and the sound reverberates through the air. The Welsh team is here to win, with the crowd behind them.

It's hard to imagine what this must have been like, when singing national anthems is now the norm before any international sporting fixture. This was the first time it had happened, and the power of thousands of Welsh voices rising above the teams would have been overwhelming.

New Zealand played poorly in the first half, and Wales scored a try. In the second half, things picked up for the All Blacks, but they did not score. Some Kiwis disagree, but the official end-of-match score was 3–0.

Since that first match, the Welsh men's team has only twice beaten the All Blacks, who have been victorious since 1953. Now, international matches are played in the Principality Stadium next door, but the legend of Gwyn Nicholls lives on via these gates.

Address Duke Street end of Westgate Street | Getting there Several buses to Westgate Street; train to Cardiff Central | Hours Accessible 24 hours | Tip Cardiff Rugby Museum shares digital records of several objects related to Gwyn Nicholls, including his book, *The Modern Rugby Game*, and the key to the memorial gates (www.cardiffrugbymuseum.org).

49 Hamadryad Hospital

From warship to uniting nations

At the height of the Industrial Revolution, Cardiff docks were the busiest in the world, attracting ships from a diverse range of countries. Thousands of sailors arrived on these shores after long journeys, and inevitably, some were not in tip-top condition. It soon became apparent that Cardiff needed additional hospital facilities to cope with the demand.

A deal was struck with the Admiralty to use one of their ships that had reached the end of its military life. In 1866, HMS *Hamadryad* was towed to East Bute Dock and converted into a hospital. This was an ideal solution that would stop infectious diseases from sweeping through the city. All patients received their treatment free of charge, with the costs covered by a voluntary fee levied on shipping. A vast majority of patients were from overseas, and all were men. Despite this being the only infectious diseases hospital in Cardiff, no women were treated on board, although plenty served as nurses. Woe betide any woman who caught an infectious disease during this period!

In its second year of operation, the hospital ship was moved to the old sea lock at the mouth of the River Taff, where it stayed for the rest of its life. By the end of the 1890s, over 10,000 people were being treated each year, and the ship was beginning to disintegrate. It was no longer fit for purpose.

The Royal Hamadryad Hospital was built on land nearby and opened in 1905. It continued to provide free treatment to seafarers until the formation of the NHS, when it became a general hospital. The ballast was removed from the hull of HMS *Hamadryad*, and a channel was dug through the muddy estuary to ease her final journey to Devon, where she was broken up. The era of a warship hospital in Cardiff was over, and all that remains of HMS *Hamadryad* are her figurehead and ship's bell, both in Amgueddfa Cymru – the National Museum of Wales.

Address Hamadryad Road, Cardiff, CF10 5UY | Getting there Several buses to Pomeroy Street | Hours Viewable from the outside only | Tip Neighbouring Hamadryad Park is a good place for a riverside stroll and also has a children's play area.

50 Hard Lines Cafe

The hottest coffee in town

From a distance, the Hard Lines Cafe does not look like anything special. On the ground floor of a modern apartment block, it would not win any architectural awards. But get close enough to look through the windows, and you can see that something different is going on. Bags of coffee and other merchandise are all emblazoned with a cartoon smiley face. And the smile doesn't end there. This café considers itself to be part of the local, national and global community.

One example of this is their Run Club, which started as a virtual club to support and stay in touch with their customers during the pandemic lockdowns. They noticed that women's attendance dropped during the winter months and asked why. Around 70 per cent of their female runners said they felt unsafe running alone in the dark, compared to 0 per cent (yes, none!) of their male runners. That fear means that many women stop running outside during the autumn and winter because it's dark by the time they get home from work. So, Hard Lines asked their Run Club members what would make them feel safer, and changed their procedures accordingly. They now supply head torches when it is dark, do a headcount at the beginning and end of a run and publish their route before meeting. This has successfully improved their retention rates.

Another example is their house coffee. Rather than just buying roasted coffee from wholesalers, the café buys coffee beans and roasts them in Cardiff, sometimes mixing beans into blends. The house coffee, called House Party, is from a single grower in Brazil. The café owners have met the growers and seen for themselves how they are introducing sustainable practices into their business.

This is a café with a community focus and a social conscience. Whether you are a coffee aficionado, need a breakfast burrito to assuage a hangover or want to feel safe while running, this is the place to go.

Address St Cannas Court, Cowbridge Road East, Canton, Cardiff, CF5 1GX, www.hard-lines.co.uk | Getting there Several buses to Canton Chapter Arts Centre; train to Ninian Park (11-minute walk) | Hours Mon–Fri 7.30am–4pm, Sat 8.30am–4pm, Sun 9am–4pm | Tip If you live to the north of the city, you might prefer to collect your coffee from the Hard Lines roastery, which is open from Mon–Thu (Gwaelod y Garth, CF15 8LA).

51 Hayes Island Snack Bar

From depot to dinner

As the population of Cardiff soared at the turn of the 20th century, so did the need for public transport. This was provided by electric trams operated by Cardiff Corporation, which ultimately expanded to cover the area between Roath, Roath Dock, Llandaff Fields and Gabalfa. By 1904, 131 burgundy and cream trams made 18 million passenger journeys a year. The trams were double-deckers on lines where bridges allowed, with the top deck open to the elements. Each tram had at least two members of staff dressed in smart uniforms. The motorman operated the tram, and the conductor collected fares. They were sometimes joined by inspectors, who checked that everyone who should have tickets did.

But it was not only people that needed to be transported. A thriving city has documents that need to be delivered, and shops that want to deliver goods. Between 1911 and 1941, the Corporation therefore also provided a delivery service. Cardiffians dropped their parcels at one of several depots, from where they were distributed using a team of boys who travelled on the trams. They, too, wore a uniform.

Due to a lack of resources, the state of the trams slowly deteriorated as World War II progressed. After the war, the trams were replaced by buses, which were far more flexible in terms of routes. Ironically, electric trams are now seen as a clean and efficient mode of transport, and tram trains are being reintroduced to the city.

Little evidence of the defunct tramways remains, except for the old parcel depot at Hayes Island. For this reason, the building is listed and therefore protected from demolition or removal. However, that listing does not stop the building from being used, and it has been the site of a snack bar for several decades. This popular place to grab a bite to eat is renowned for its sandwiches, hot dogs and jacket potatoes, all served in generous portions.

Address The Hayes, St David's Centre, Cardiff, CF10 1AH, +44 (0) 292 022 6699, www.facebook.com/TheHayesIslandSnackBar | Getting there Several buses to Westgate Street; train to Cardiff Central | Hours Mon–Fri 7am–5pm, Sat 7am–6pm, Sun 9am–5pm | Tip The public toilets next to the snack bar are on the listed buildings register as a good example of Victorian underground public loos.

52 Hendre Lake

What did the Romans ever do for us?

Hendre Lake is in an area known as the Wentloog Levels, which lie on the low land by the Severn Estuary between the Usk and Rhymney Rivers. From there to the River Wye, they continue as the Caldicot Levels, and together they make the Gwent Levels. Hendre Lake is a joy to visit, with a circular footpath around it, providing intermittent views of the water. The lake is stocked with fish, so is popular with anglers. It also acts as a magnet to local wildlife, especially birds, including herons, geese and swans.

When the Romans arrived in Wales in 45 A.D., this coastal area was wet and boggy, and much of it was washed by the tides twice a day. The Romans were a resourceful bunch, though, and saw potential in an area others might have considered nothing more than wasteland. They set about building a sea wall, draining it and creating long fields on which they could grow crops to support the legions at Caerleon. This area of land reclaimed by the Romans is on a scale unique to Wales and has therefore been designated as an Outstanding Landscape of Historic Interest in Wales.

After the Roman legions departed some three centuries later, the land was no longer required. However, during the medieval period, the sea wall was rebuilt, and the fields were brought back into use. In many parts of the country, fields were delineated using hedges, but here in the wetlands, the ditches used to drain the land also performed this function. The long, thin fields typical of these Roman and medieval farming systems can still be seen to the south of Hendre Lake. Some of the field boundaries also have distinctive wiggles, marking the routes of the original tidal creeks.

The sea wall is now 35 kilometres long, and the Gwent Levels have 1,500 kilometres of watercourses and ditches that are attractive to aquatic wildlife such as birds and dragonflies.

Address Cyprus Drive, St Mellons, Cardiff, CF3 0RG, www.hendrelake.co.uk | Getting there Several buses to Willowbrook School – access to lake to southwest of bus stop; on-site parking | Hours Accessible 24 hours | Tip As well as the country park surrounding the lake, there is a community garden in St Mellons, open on Fridays from 1–4pm (4a Newent Road, www.facebook.com/stmellonscommunitygarden).

53 Heroes of Wales

Black lives matter

Most people born after 2015 will never forget 2020. It was, of course, the year of the Coronavirus pandemic. It was also the year in which the Black Lives Matter movement catapulted into the public consciousness in the UK, and on 7 June, an angry crowd in Bristol toppled the statue of Edward Colston off its plinth and into the dock.

Cardiff City Council quickly identified the statue of Sir Thomas Picton, one of the Heroes of Wales standing in City Hall, as contentious, consulted the public and held a vote on whether to retain or remove it. The Heroes of Wales statues were initially chosen by public vote early in the 20th century and unveiled in 1916. Sir Thomas Picton was included in the shortlist because he was the highest-ranking officer killed at the Battle of Waterloo in 1815. However, even when he was alive, he was a contentious figure, and many people considered his behaviour to be unacceptable. He gained the unenviable nickname of the 'Tyrant of Trinidad' when he was the governor, and was tried for the torture of Louisa Calderon, a 14-year-old girl, a crime for which he was convicted in 1806.

Cardiff City Council has apologised for including Picton in the original shortlist, and councillors overwhelmingly voted for the removal of the statue. Shortly afterwards, it was boarded up, and the council was given planning permission to remove it.

There remains some debate about whether contentious statues should be removed or left in place and put into historical context. Some would like to see them replaced with statues that better represent positive aspects of our history. Others would like to see the removal of all statues of people, given that no outstanding achievements are made as an entirely solo endeavour. The debate has at least encouraged us to learn more about our history, good and bad, and to consider how to right historic wrongs.

Address Cardiff City Hall, King Edward VII Avenue, Cardiff, CF10 3ND, www.cardiffcityhall.com, cityhall@cardiff.gov.uk | Getting there Several buses to Greyfriars Road Stop GN, Kingsway Hilton stop GP or Law Courts Stop RJ; train to Cathays | Hours See website for current information on visiting | Tip A walk around the surrounding Civic Quarter will reveal many buildings that give an indication of the wealth generated locally during the Industrial Revolution.

54 Ianto's Shrine

Fans forever

When BBC screenwriters killed off Ianto Jones from the TV series *Torchwood*, there was uproar in the fan community. A campaign was launched to resurrect the character, resulting in more than 7,600 emails being sent to the BBC. Images appeared of Ianto in tourist destinations, in an attempt to show that he was just travelling, not dead after all, and his character could therefore be resurrected. The emails, letters, coffee and photos sent to the BBC did not prove to be successful, but the memory of Ianto lives on at Mermaid Quay.

Torchwood (an anagram of 'Doctor Who') was a spin-off from the *Doctor Who* series, aired between 2006 and 2011 and aimed at a more adult audience. It became a hit in both the UK and the US. The plot involved a team of alien hunters based in Cardiff, who protected humans from a series of extraterrestrial threats. In the early episodes, Ianto was a supporting character providing coffee and other essential services to the alien-hunting team. However, as the series developed, so did the character. He became a fully fledged alien hunter, loved by the audience for his witty one-liners and maybe his very human obsession with coffee, too.

Over time, he became the romantic interest of the lead character, Captain Jack Harkness, while also having a relationship with Lisa, a woman-turned-half-cyborg. Some believe it is this romantic entanglement that heightened the sense of grief felt by the show's fans. Having watched the relationship between Jack and Ianto grow after Lisa's death, the storyline was dramatically severed with no real conclusion.

It is unknown who started the shrine to Ianto, but once one dedication had been left, it opened the floodgates. Flowers, photos, teddy bears and coffee cups appeared by the dozen. The Mermaid Quay management team had a choice: tidy it up or look after it. They chose the latter, and 15 years later, the shrine lives on.

Address Tacoma Square, Cardiff, CF10 5BZ | Getting there Train to Cardiff Bay; bus 1, 1A, 8 or X2 to Mermaid Quay | Hours Accessible 24 hours | Tip The entrance to Torchwood's headquarters is at the base of the columnar fountain in Roald Dahl Plass, in front of the Millennium Centre.

55 Insole Court

Keeping up with the Butes, but not the times

In Victorian times, standing in society was everything, and James Hardy Insole went to great lengths to prove his gentlemanly status. It was not the Joneses that he tried to keep up with, but the Butes – the wealthiest and most influential family in the Cardiff area.

George Insole made his fortune from the Rhondda coal mines, and when he died in 1840, James Hardy Insole inherited it. He continued to operate mines, build the family's wealth and buy landholdings. In 1856, apparently due to his wilful negligence, one of his collieries at Cymmer suffered the largest mining disaster yet known. In the same year, he started to build Insole Court, perhaps in an attempt to repair any loss of social standing with the Cardiff elite. This was a mansion that was designed to elevate his standing. He commissioned a tower for the house that emulated the clock tower at Cardiff Castle in style, if not in stature. He used alabaster from Penarth, as the castle's architect did, and he commissioned a similar frieze for the drawing room to one in the castle. Even the large pleasure garden with its exotic trees was a symbol of wealth and status.

As fashions changed, so did the house. By Edwardian times, the Gothic Revival style of the tower and some other parts of the house was considered gaudy. The tower was reduced in height, and the heavily decorated library ceiling was covered over by that seen today.

As the use of coal plummeted, so did the family's finances. They suffered from the classic issue of the third generation spending the family's fortune and not adapting the business to keep up with the times. In 1938, ownership of the house was transferred to the state, and it is now looked after by a charity. Although the downstairs rooms of the house are open to the public free of charge, the guided tour, which takes in more of the house and reveals more of its secrets, is recommended.

Address Fairwater Road, Llandaff, Cardiff, CF5 2LN, +44 (0) 292 116 7920, www.insolecourt.org, enquiry@insolecourt.org | Getting there Bus 25, 62, 63, 122 or 124 to Llandaff Black Lion; train to Fairwater | Hours House daily 10am–4pm; garden daily dawn–dusk | Tip Guided tours of the clock tower at Cardiff Castle are available from March to October (www.cardiffcastle.com).

56 Irbic's Cross

Interlaced history

The stone pillar cross that stands in St Dochdwy's churchyard in Llandough could be considered to be pretty ancient, at around 1,000 years old. However, this site, on the fertile lowlands of the Vale of Glamorgan, has been occupied for even longer than that.

A round building once stood to one side of where the church is now, followed by a villa built by the Romans. Around 200 years after the Romans left, St Dochdwy established a monastery in the same place. As Llandough is so close to Dinas Powis, it is likely that the monastery was linked to the high-status person who occupied the hillfort, and that it was established with their permission. The size of the cemetery, with 1,026 burials, and well established by the 6th century, suggests that this was an important early Medieval monastery.

The cross is comparatively new, dating from the late 10th or early 11th century. This was around the time that Llandaff was adopted as the seat of a bishop. When that happened, the status of Llandaff Cathedral needed a boost, and the church at Llandough proved a valuable source of material. St Dochdwy's became far less important, and by the end of the 11th century, it had lost its monastic status. The cross is carved from local limestone, which has weathered remarkably well over the centuries, allowing the intricate details of the carvings to remain visible. It is inscribed IRBIC, which is thought to be a name. It is also decorated with a horseman, five standing figures, two busts and a Celtic knot pattern. The knot pattern is known as 'interlace', and although most keenly associated with the Celts, it was also used by the Romans in mosaic floors.

The cross at St Dochdwy's is almost complete. A fragment of carved stone with a remarkably similar pattern was found at Llandaff, and given the relationship between the two sites, it is possible that the fragment is the missing piece.

Address St Dochdwy's Church, Leckwith Road, Llandough, Cardiff, CF64 2LL, www.parishofpenarthandllandough.co.uk | **Getting there** Bus 95 to Llandough Institute; train to Cogan (21-minute walk) | **Hours** Accessible 24 hours | **Tip** Cardiff-based Alex Waddell is a stone carver who accepts commissions and runs courses at his workshop in Adamsdown (www.alexwaddellcarver.com).

57 Ivor Novello Statue

Keep the home fires burning

Ivor Novello was not a novelist, as his name suggests, but a playwright, composer and actor. Born David Ivor Davies in Cardiff in 1893, he was heavily influenced by his mother, who was a world-renowned singing teacher and choral conductor. He combined his middle name with hers to create his professional name Ivor Novello.

At the age of 20, he moved to London with his mother, who was working as a voice coach. They lived in a flat above the Strand Theatre, which he would maintain for the rest of his life. The Strand Theatre was renamed the Ivor Novello Theatre in 2005.

Ivor Novello was only 21 when World War I broke out. Before he joined up, the pain of war inspired him to compose the music for 'Keep the Home Fires Burning', a popular song that helped to maintain morale among the troops. When he enlisted into the Royal Naval Air Service, his flying skills did not match his musical skills, and after crashing two of their planes, he was given an office job in London.

After the war, he extended his repertoire to acting in and writing plays. During the 1920s, he was a popular film star and stage actor. He gained a reputation for being outrageous, and the parties he threw at his house in Maidenhead were legendary. His unconventional behaviour continued into World War II when he was too old to serve in the forces. Instead, he served a short prison term for abusing fuel vouchers.

This did not stop the British public from adoring him and his work. His 1951 musical, *King's Rhapsody*, was just what people needed to lift their spirits after the deprivations of the war years and those immediately following. He was still performing in this show when he died from a heart attack at the age of 58. However, his legacy lives on and he is remembered in several parts of the country, including here in Cardiff, the place of his birth.

Address Roald Dahl Plass, Cardiff, CF10 4PZ | Getting there Several buses to Millennium Centre; train to Cardiff Bay | Hours Accessible 24 hours | Tip Cross the road at the north end of Roald Dahl Plass to see a statue of a somewhat more restrained figure – Mahatma Gandhi.

58 Jake's Kingdom

Perched in the past

In the winter of 2010–2011, snow lay across the UK for several weeks. It was during this period that Ian, the owner of Jacobs Antiques Centre, heard a forlorn peeping coming from behind a plant pot outside the shop. He investigated and found a small cockatiel hunkered down, sheltering from the worst of the weather.

Cockatiels are native to Australia and not used to such wintry conditions, so it's no surprise that he was unhappy. Ian scooped him up, warmed him up and started to look after him. The newly named Jake thrived in his new environment and is now the star of the antiques centre. The average lifespan of a wild cockatiel is 12 to 15 years; however, in ideal conditions in captivity, they can live for up to 25 years. Jake is free to fly around the antiques centre and out of the front door if he so chooses. However, he knows how unpleasant the outside world can be and tends to stick to his own territory, around the large bird cage.

Jacobs has been an antiques centre for over 40 years. Before then, it was a timber yard, and when it was built, it was a wholesaler's. Over 30 stalls selling art and vintage and antique goods operate across three storeys of the building. A small coffee shop provides hot drinks and pastries during the day. In the evening, the cellar converts into a rave venue, popular with techno and house-music fans. The newest space in the building is at the very top of the stairs. Here, there is a quiet roof garden with views across to the modern towers of the city centre. Although the area is small, it feels spacious because of its airiness. During the day, it is quiet, but at night, it transforms into another music venue.

This building and the people who operate stalls in it have adapted over time as needs have dictated. No doubt they will continue to do so, with Jake overseeing it all, hopefully for many years to come.

Address W Canal Wharf, Cardiff, CF10 5DB, +44 (0) 292 039 0939, www.jacobsmarket.co.uk | **Getting there** Train to Cardiff Central; bus 304 or X2 to Tresillian Way | **Hours** Thu–Sat 9.30am–5pm | **Tip** For less lofty gardens, head across St Mary Street to Callaghan Square, a modern park with ponds, fountains and benches.

59 Llanrumney Hall

Sweet as sugar?

Llanrumney was once a village, but has now been subsumed by Cardiff. You might also see the name if you ever travel to Jamaica. The link? A man whose family owned Llanrumney Hall in the 17th century – Sir Henry Morgan. You might expect that someone who was knighted and became the Governor of Jamaica would be a man of honour, but in this case, it is just the opposite, judged by the moral standards of today's society.

Back then, people were rewarded for what we now consider abominable behaviour. A fine line may exist on paper between 'privateering' and 'piracy', but the only real difference is that the first is authorised by a head of state. The result is much the same: ships and cities are attacked, plundered and captured. People kill, all manner of people lose their lives, and all for the opportunity to amass a fortune and a reputation as a patriot. Henry Morgan was involved in this activity and took a step too far when he attacked Panama shortly after the English and Spanish governments had signed a peace accord. He was arrested and repatriated to London. However, that was not the end of his story – a couple of years later, he was back in favour, and the king knighted him. He returned to Jamaica as deputy to the Governor and served as Governor for a short period himself.

Despite the peace accord, Sir Henry Morgan continued to benefit from investing in privateers/pirates – he just had to be more underhand about his methods. He further indulged the unsavoury side of his character through enslavement – by the time he died, he owned three sugar plantations, along with title to 131 African men, women and children.

These days, Llanrumney Hall has shaken off its ties to enslavement and piracy. Instead, it is run by a community-led trust to provide a support hub to the people of East Cardiff, helping to eradicate poverty and provide opportunities to local people.

Address Ball Road, Llanrumney, Cardiff, CF3 4JJ, +44 (0) 292 000 1441, www.llanrumneyhall.org, info@llanrumneyhall.org | Getting there Bus 50 or 101 to Llanrumney Hall; parking on site or nearby | Hours Viewable from the outside 24 hours; see website for information on events | Tip On the hill above Llanrumney Hall, Fishpond Wood has paths across the fields and through the woods.

60 Lloyd George Avenue

A path to Parliament

Towards the end of the 20th century, the architects of the Cardiff Bay development envisaged a continental-style boulevard transforming the industrial dereliction of Butetown and transporting people between the city centre and the bay. The train line would be replaced by light tram-trains running along the middle of the boulevard, which would be flanked by a matching avenue of trees on each side. During the development process, compromises were made, and the vision was not fully realised. The dereliction has been transformed, but there is only one avenue of trees, with the old railway still creating a hard boundary on the far side of the road. However, the trees already provide some shelter from summer sun and rain showers, and public art lines the path.

Initially, the boulevard was called 'Bute Avenue' in recognition of the role of the Bute family in turning Cardiff from a small town into an Industrial Revolution powerhouse. However, it now sports the name of someone who was possibly equally as influential in the history of Cardiff: David Lloyd George.

Lloyd George grew up in North Wales as a native Welsh speaker in a household with strong political ideals. For 55 years, he served as a Member of Parliament for Caernarvon Burrows, and for six of those he was Prime Minister of the UK. The relevance to Cardiff? He was a strong proponent of Welsh devolution and campaigned for such from as early as 1880. Unfortunately, he did not live to see his vision come to fruition over a century later. He would have been delighted to have seen Wales accepted as a country in its own right and get its own capital city, although he might have preferred Caernarfon over Cardiff. He would have been even more delighted to have seen devolution happen. It is, therefore, fitting that this road, leading from the centre of Cardiff to the home of the Welsh Parliament, should bear his name.

Address Lloyd George Avenue, Cardiff, CF10 4DB | Getting there Bus X2 or 304 to Callaghan Square at one end or several buses to Millennium Centre at the other; train to Cardiff Bay | Hours Accessible 24 hours | Tip Callaghan Square, at the north end of Lloyd George Avenue, is named after another Prime Minister of the UK, Lord Callaghan, who was also the MP for Cardiff South and Penarth.

61 Mansion House

Designed for downsizing

In Wales, tens of thousands of people are waiting for housing, and thousands live in temporary accommodation. To resolve this situation, there has been a significant focus on reducing the attractiveness of second homes and building new houses to increase supply. One issue that is occasionally raised is that of one or two people continuing to live in a large family home, sometimes despite the difficulties and costs of doing so. Understandably, people do not want to leave a house that is full of memories or a neighbourhood that is familiar and full of friends and social networks.

One solution is to split an existing home into smaller units. Some companies are now constructing new homes that are designed to be reconfigured, either combining apartments into larger houses or splitting houses into flats or smaller units. This sort of forward planning might be attributed to modern buildings. However, it is not such a new phenomenon.

Mansion House, initially called Grove House, was built for James Howell, the founder of Howells department store, at the end of the 19th century. When specifying his requirements for his new residence, James Howell was already thinking about what would happen to the house when he died. The magnificent, wide staircase leading from a grand hallway with a pair of front doors adjacent to each other provides a clue about his plans. The house was designed to be easily split into two by adding a wall starting between the front doors and running up the middle of the staircase. Although half the width of the original, the split staircase would still be impressive. The plans to divide the house never came to fruition, as it was bought by the Cardiff Corporation after his death. Its name was changed to Mansion House, and it became the Lord Mayor's official residence. Since then, guests have included royalty, heads of state and even Hollywood stars.

Address Richmond Road, Cardiff, CF24 3UN | **Getting there** Several buses to Richmond Crescent; train to Cardiff Queen Street or Cathays | **Hours** Viewable from the outside only | **Tip** To experience a night in a luxurious mansion yourself, try the New House Country Hotel in Thornhill, where guests step into the shoes of the wealthy 18th-century industrialist whose home it was (www.townandcountrycollective.co.uk/new-house-home).

62 Marments Monograms

Shop 'til you drop

Department stores are now a thing of the past on many high streets. However, they were once the height of fashion. Towards the end of the 18th century and early in the 19th, the Industrial Revolution caused the growth of the middle class. Aspirations rose alongside incomes, and the concept of shopping as a leisure activity was born.

As an alternative to shopping on dirty and possibly unsafe streets, the department stores that sprang up in every major town gave women somewhere comfortable and exciting they could go without a male escort. Especially after Harry Gordon Selfridge brought glitzy ideas to the UK from the US, department stores were seen not just as somewhere to shop but as destinations in their own right. Designs were lavish, and departments in which to eat, drink and rest were added to those in which to shop.

The departments tell you something about life at the time – the first London department store sold furs and fans, haberdashery, watches, clocks and millinery. By the late 20th century, departments usually included luggage for package holidays, kitchenware and furniture, alongside clothes, jewellery and perfume.

Marments department store opened on Duke Street in Cardiff in 1879. It was immediately popular and quickly expanded. When the road was widened in 1923, the store moved to this site on Queen Street, and included 15 departments and 140 staff. By 1986, competition in the form of shopping malls and out-of-town retail developments forced the Marment family to close the business.

Internet shopping has added to the competitive landscape, and department stores have largely disappeared from all our town centres. The only clues that Marments once stood here are the carved monograms of the letters L and M on the wall facing the pavement, and the impressive fluted Roman Doric columns supporting the upper levels.

Address Unit 13, Queen Street, Cardiff, CF10 2AQ | Getting there Several buses to Kingsway or Castle stops; train to Cardiff Central or Cathays | Hours Accessible 24 hours | Tip There are several other interesting carvings on the façades of Queen Street, including an elephant's head above what is now Starbucks.

63 Medieval Walls

Fire, flood and fortification

This section of wall doesn't look like much now, but it is the largest remaining part of the structure that kept Cardiffians safe in medieval times. You can tell from the size of the stones that this was not meant to defend against military forces, evidenced during Owain Glyndŵr's revolt of 1403, when the wall and town suffered significant damage.

Instead, it was built to keep raiders out at night. In the Middle Ages, Cardiff was a small town where everyone knew each other. Six gates allowed visitors to enter the town during the day, but when the church bells signalled curfew, the gates were closed. This allowed townspeople to sleep easy, knowing that casual troublemakers would not gain entry. Of course, this did not deal with all threats.

The houses were built from wattle, daubed with clay dug from a pit in Cathays, and topped with thatch. They were built in rows, which could lead to fire spreading quickly from house to house and engulfing the entire town. To avert a disaster, watchmen patrolled the streets at night. If they spotted a fire, they used the church bells to ring an alarm. This would bring all the residents running to tackle it together, handing buckets of water along a line to dampen the flames and pulling down burning thatch and timbers to stop the fire from spreading.

Being so close to the river and sea meant that flooding could also be an issue, and it is thought that the walls nearest to the water were undermined and collapsed due to its power. In contrast, when the River Taff flowed gently, people would paddle onto it in coracles to fish.

Although the buildings were close to each other, there was also plenty of space for plants and trees. Even the wealthy artisans and traders grew or raised much of their own food, and the smartest gardens were bordered by hedges, or 'hayes', after which one of the main streets is still named (The Hayes).

Address Behind Northgate House Apartments, Kingsway, Cardiff, CF10 3FD | Getting there Several buses to Kingsway or Castle stops; train to Cardiff Central or Cathays | Hours Accessible 24 hours | Tip On returning to the road, look ahead and to the left to see another, smaller section of the wall near the castle.

64 Melingriffith Water Pump

A century of revolution

When the Glamorganshire Canal was first built to transport iron from Merthyr Tydfil into Cardiff, an agreement was reached that it would not impinge on the water supply of any local industry. By the time the canal got close to Cardiff, it needed topping up, and the lock at Melingriffith was initially supplied from a feeder channel from Radyr Weir. The same feeder was also used by the local tinplate works, which was the largest in the world at the time. During dry spells, this meant that the tinplate works had to stop production due to lack of water. Understandably, the owners did not take kindly to this disruption of their manufacturing process. A legal battle ensued, resulting in an agreement that the canal would pump water from the works' tailrace instead of its headrace, thus causing no impediment to operations.

This was to be done with a new pump, now known as the Melingriffith water pump, which was first operational in 1793. An undershot water-wheel-powered cylinder pumps that lifted water almost four metres up to the level of the canal. The canal owners were key players in the Industrial Revolution that enabled steam power to be used, rather than relying on water wheels. It was a little incongruous to fill their canals using a water wheel, so they tried to upgrade the pump to run on steam. However, the owners of the tinplate works were not happy with the additional cost it would entail for them, so the water-wheel-powered pump continued in use.

It is thought to have been replaced once by an upgraded model, but other than that, it operated continuously for over 130 years until 1927, by which time the ironworks had closed and the canal was no longer needed.

The tinplate works remained in business until 1957, and the site has since become a housing estate. The wheel has been restored twice, but it has not been operational since 2016.

Address Ty-Mawr Road, Whitchurch, Cardiff, CF14 2BH | Getting there Train to Llandaff Station (13-minute walk); bus 25, 101 or 102 to Velindre Hospital (12-minute walk) | Hours Accessible 24 hours | Tip The City of Cardiff (Melingriffith) Brass Band, which was associated with the tinplate works, has outlasted its host and still performs (www.melingriffith.co.uk).

65 Melingriffith Wild Swimming

Where water works wonders

On the outskirts of Cardiff, just beyond Llandaff station, the Taff winds through a valley bounded by woods and fields. The meanders encourage deposition of stones on the inside edge of the bend. Immediately downstream of the railway bridge, this creates an ideal spot for a dip.

The river is shallow at the edge, allowing you to enter the water slowly and get your body used to the temperature. In the UK, wild swimming is known as cold-water swimming for a reason! Entering slowly also lets you get a feel for the current before you commit. Of course, the river's flow will depend on how much rain has fallen recently, so it will be different each time you go.

The increase in the popularity of wild swimming has led to more research on its health benefits. And it seems there are many, both physical and mental, a good number of which we don't yet understand. How can immersion in cold water reduce depression? How can it have a positive impact on your immune system when getting cold normally weakens it? There is much still to be learnt. However, the benefits are clearly real.

Other research has shown that many people are wary of swimming because they fear pollution in our waterways. Although this can be an issue – and it's always a good idea to be alert to odd smells and the appearance of the water – it is rare for wild swimmers to be made ill by it. It seems that others are wary because they believe that wild swimming means swimming in the nude. That is not the case; wild swimming is any swimming in open water, however dressed or undressed you choose to be.

Look online for advice about how to stay safe in the water and how to warm up afterwards. The Outdoor Swimming Society has guidance on its website (www.outdoorswimmingsociety.com), as do other organisations such as Swim Wales.

Address Entry to site from Ty-Mawr Road, Whitchurch, Cardiff, CF14 2BH | Getting there Train to Llandaff Station (13-minute walk); bus 25, 101 or 102 to Velindre Hospital (12-minute walk) | Hours Accessible 24 hours | Tip If you prefer swimming in a pool with lifeguards, try Fairwater Leisure Centre nearby (off Waterhall Road, Fairwater, CF5 3LL, www.better.org.uk).

66 Memorial to Merchant Seafarers

Hidden heroes

'Merchant Navy' is a term coined during World War I in recognition of the valuable and risky work that those employed on merchant ships did. During the two world wars, these ships and their personnel were not a part of the armed forces but provided essential support in transporting troops and supplies around the world. They therefore became a target of enemy efforts to sever supply lines. Ships sailed together in convoy, with a military escort to reduce the risk of attack. The risk was not removed entirely – a higher proportion of members of the Merchant Navy died in World War II than those of any of the armed forces.

The variety of people on board a merchant vessel was also wider than those in the armed forces. Teenagers were permitted to serve on ships, as were women and older people. People from around the world served in the British Merchant Navy, including many from India, China and West African countries.

Kenneth James Lewis and his older brother Raymond Leslie were both on the S.S. (Steam Ship) *Fiscus*, a Cardiff ship, on 18 October, 1940, when it was attacked. At the ages of 14 and 15, they were extremely young to be serving in an arena of war. In addition to children, almost 50 female members of the Merchant Navy died during the war as a result of enemy action, alongside people from across the world.

As an area that provided a significant number of ships and personnel to the Merchant Navy, it seems appropriate that the merchant seafarers from the ports of Barry, Penarth and Cardiff are remembered here on Cardiff Bay. At first glance, the memorial may simply appear to be a beached ship. Look more closely, and you will see a sleeping face built into the hull. The memorial was created by Brian Fell, whose father served in the Merchant Navy in World War II.

Address Harbour Drive, Cardiff, CF99 1SN | Getting there Train to Cardiff Bay; bus 1, 1A, 8 or X2 to Mermaid Quay | Hours Accessible 24 hours | Tip John Masefield celebrates shipping in a different way in his poem 'Cargoes'. Walk for 155 metres with the bay on your left to read his poem and see whether you can find the 21 sculptures that represent it in Mermaid Quay.

67 Millennium Centre Façade

An allegorical elevation

The façade of the Millennium Centre is familiar to everyone in Cardiff and many around the world. It is bold, striking, and some might even say iconic. But it is more than that; there are layers of meaning built into the structure that are perhaps not immediately evident.

Let's start with the poem, cut into the metallic frontage. The English part refers to stones and singing, and it's easy to see how this relates to a concert venue. The reference to horizons holds connotations of something beyond the local; of an international context to the work performed here. Those who don't speak Welsh may not realise that the Welsh words say something different. They refer to Wales' industrial and cultural heritage. The copper-coloured building reminded the poet of Ceridwen's cauldron, which grants poetic inspiration, wisdom and transformation (*awen* in Welsh) in the *Tale of Taliesin*. The reference to a furnace brings it into the modern age.

The font used for the words was created specifically for this building, representing the uniqueness and artistic excellence of the cultural offering made here. It was designed to look like letters carved into stones, reflecting Wales' Roman and Celtic history.

The whole of Wales is represented in the materials chosen for the building. The layers of slate represent one of the most significant industries of North Wales. They are also designed to look like the layered cliffs of South Wales. The roof is made from steel, representing one of the most important industries of South Wales. And, although the building is sometimes referred to as 'The Armadillo', it was designed to look like a ship's hull, reflecting the importance of ports and shipping in the country's development.

Familiar, yet with layers of meaning, the Millennium Centre façade hints at the rich seam of Wales' culture and history, in whose context modern shows are performed.

Address Roald Dahl Plass, Cardiff, CF10 4PZ | **Getting there** Train to Cardiff Bay; Baycar 6 to Millennium Centre; bus 1, 8 or X2 to Mermaid Quay | **Hours** Accessible 24 hours | **Tip** For an intimate venue that focuses on experimental performance and other art forms, head over to Chapter in Canton (www.chapter.org).

68 Million-Pound Trading Floor

The golden years of coal

Around the turn of the 20th century, the port of Cardiff was the busiest in the world. Steam had superseded sail, and oil had not yet been found in commercial quantities, so coal was king, and exported through Cardiff in record quantities to fuel the Industrial Revolution. The docks were busy, and trades between mine owners and shipowners and their agents were growing in volume and frequency. It was time to stop meeting on the dockside or in a pub during inclement weather. It made sense to move the trades into a purpose-made building.

During the middle of the 19th century, Mount Stuart Square was a fashionable neighbourhood for wealthy professionals. However, as the area became more industrialised, they moved out. It was the ideal place, then, to build a coal and shipping exchange similar to those already opened in London, Liverpool and Manchester.

Every day, the trading floor of the coal and shipping hall would fill with coal owners, shipowners and their agents, noisily doing deals. They swapped their oilskins for top hats, morning coats and spats over well-polished shoes. During the busiest periods, there would be up to 200 people raising their voices to make themselves heard. Luckily, there were wine merchants on the balcony, so lucrative deals could be celebrated and sore throats soothed with a bottle of something bubbly.

It was here on the trading floor in the early years of the 20th century that the world's first £1 million deal was struck, securing Cardiff's place in the economic hall of fame. Since the decline of the coal industry from the middle of the 20th century, the building has suffered variable fortune. For now, the proprietors of the Coal Exchange Hotel are doing their best to keep the building not only in use but maintained and further renovated, as an architectural and historical gem.

Address Coal Exchange Hotel, Mount Stuart Square, Cardiff, CF10 5FQ, +44 (0) 292 199 1904, www.coalexchangecardiff.co.uk, info@coalexchangecardiff.co.uk | **Getting there** Bus 304 or 305 to Mount Stuart Square; train to Cardiff Bay | **Hours** Accessible 24 hours | **Tip** The hotel is not far from the River Taff or Cardiff Bay. Head west to the river, then turn left before the bridge and follow the edge of the water round to the waterfront. Turn back inland to the hotel for a lovely circular walk.

69 Mrs Pratchett's Sweet Shop

Scene of The Great Mouse Plot

From his novels, such as *James and the Giant Peach* and *Matilda*, Roald Dahl was blatantly a man of great imagination who was not concerned with the practicalities of health and safety. It seems he was also a *boy* of great imagination with little concern for health and safety.

When he and his friends found a loose floorboard at the back of their classroom, they thought this would be the ideal place to hide any treasures they found, such as sweets or conkers. One day, when they lifted the floorboard, they were greeted by an unpleasant smell that was emanating from a dead mouse. At first, they were not sure what to do with it, but then Roald had an idea.

He dropped the mouse into his trouser pocket, and after school, the group headed for the sweet shop in Llandaff. The owner was in her seventies by the time Roald Dahl was a pupil at the Cathedral School, and probably thought she had seen it all from her ebullient customers. Hearts pounding, Roald Dahl and his friends entered and enacted their plan. One of the others distracted the shopkeeper by asking for a sweet. As soon as she turned to reach for it, Roald lifted the lid of the gobstopper jar and transferred the decomposing mouse into its new home. The shopkeeper did not yet know what he had done, but she shouted at them to leave because only one had bought any sweets. This gave them the excuse they needed, and they ran.

They might have thought they had got away with it, but of course, the shopkeeper soon noticed the dead mouse in one of her jars and guessed exactly who was behind the prank. In those days, corporal punishment was still permitted, and Roald Dahl was given a caning by the school authorities. Luckily, this had no discernible impact on his imagination, and his stories, at least one of which was inspired by his sweet-eating days, have entertained multiple generations of children ever since.

Address 11 High Street, Llandaff, Cardiff, CF5 2DX | **Getting there** Bus 24, 62, 63 or M1 to Black Lion; train to Fairwater (15-minute walk) | **Hours** Viewable from the outside only (no longer a shop) | **Tip** There is no longer a sweet shop in Llandaff. However, if you have a sweet tooth, you could try Coffi Lab café, a few doors back along the High Street, which sells cakes and pastries as well as coffee.

70 New Theatre

Stage lights and spectres

Theatregoers want to feel some sort of emotion – perhaps the joy of listening to sublime music, the hilarity of a farce, the energy of an upbeat musical or the terror of a psychological thriller. Some even go to the theatre for a good old cry. But no one wants the sort of emotion that one visitor experienced.

Imagine her shock as she looked around the auditorium and saw her partner sitting in a box with another woman. Imagine her heart sinking as she worked through different scenarios and concluded this must be a love affair. In a state of distress, she turned on her heel and unthinkingly fled the auditorium, down the stairs, out of a side entrance and into the road. Tragically, she darted out just as a horse and cart was passing. She was hit. And killed. It is said that her ghost still haunts the building, moving objects, slamming and locking doors, and leaving a trail of chilled air in her wake.

When it was opened in 1906, the New Theatre had one of the largest stages in Wales. The original building has been added to, neglected, and refurbished several times since then. It has been used for musical theatre and drama and was the home of Welsh National Opera for 50 years before they moved to the Millennium Centre. Shirley Bassey sang here in one of her first professional shows – *Hot from Harlem* – and Anthony Hopkins unveiled the bust of the author and broadcaster Gwyn Thomas that sits in the foyer. The theatre has also been used for radio broadcasting and showing films, and it was the final venue of the Prince of Wales' post-investiture tour in 1969.

The original parts of the Grade II-listed building and its striking façade, with turrets and cupolas, are made from red brick with Bath stone dressings. The foundation stone can be seen in the foyer, and if you catch the theatre director at the right time, he might even have the very trowel used to lay it tucked into his pocket.

Address Park Place, Cardiff, CF10 3LN, www.trafalgartickets.com | Getting there Several buses to Greyfriars Road; train to Cardiff Queen Street | Hours Outside accessible 24 hours; see website for current information on shows | Tip For shows with a Welsh flavour, check out the programme at the Sherman Theatre (Senghennydd Road, CF24 4YE, www.shermantheatre.co.uk).

71 Norwegian Church

Pit props and pulpits

The growing number and size of coal mines in South Wales in the 18th century created an increased demand for wood that could be used as pit props. By the 19th century, no local supplies remained, and timber had to be imported for this purpose. Scandinavia, on the other hand, was producing plenty of wood for export and needed coal. This led to a growing number of Scandinavian ships visiting South Wales ports, including Cardiff, each with a complement of Scandinavian seafarers. In 1869, the Norwegian Seamen's Mission built a church on Cardiff Docks to support their countrymen.

With up to 90 Norwegian vessels docked in Cardiff at any one time, the church thrived. As Norwegian seafarers settled in Cardiff, the congregation grew to include families, including the Dahls, whose son Roald was baptised in the church. The church played a crucial role in maintaining Norwegian cultural ties and providing a support network for the growing expatriate community.

However, as the coal industry declined, so did the congregation, and the Seamen's Mission left in 1959. By 1987, the structure was in a perilous state, so it was dismantled and put into storage while locals, including Roald Dahl, fought for its survival. In 1992, it was re-erected in its current position. It is now run by a charity as an arts centre, café and events space, preserving its heritage while serving a new purpose in the community.

Sjømanns Kirken (Seaman's Church) continues to support Norwegians living, working or travelling outside Norway. They currently operate 28 churches and have chaplains in around 80 countries. They also visit Norwegian ships and oil rigs in the North Sea. This global network reflects the ongoing importance attached to providing spiritual and cultural support to Norwegians abroad, a mission that began with churches like this one in Cardiff over 150 years ago.

Address Harbour Drive, Cardiff Bay, Cardiff, CF10 4PA, +44 (0) 292 049 2261, www.norwegianchurchcardiff.com | Getting there Bus 1, 1A or 8 to Mermaid Quay; train to Cardiff Bay | Hours Daily 10.30am–6pm | Tip For more Scandinavian food, there are several branches of BRØD Danish bakery in Cardiff. The nearest is at 18 James Street, CF10 5EX (www.thedanishbakery.co.uk).

72 Old Baths, Penarth

A pool of champions

It's not surprising to learn that water polo is a sport that the Welsh excelled in when it was introduced, as it is based on the game of rugby. Initially, it was a serious contact sport, with the underwater wrestling as entertaining as the official game. However, by the time the Penarth Swimming and Water Polo Club started to play in the baths on Penarth promenade, the refinement of the sport had started.

The baths opened in 1885 to cater to the burgeoning population in the area. Seawater was pumped up from the shore and filtered before being added to the pools. It was another 25 years before swimming pools started to be treated with chlorine.

Over 100 people joined the club within its first year, and it was in water polo that the members excelled. The sporting greats who played for Penarth include Paul Radmilovic, who was born in Tiger Bay. At just 15, in 1901, he became the youngest-ever international player. He went on to win four Olympic gold medals in a combination of swimming and water polo, a record that was not beaten until Sir Steve Redgrave won his fifth in the 2000 Sydney Olympics.

Gus Taylor was another member of the club. He captained the team before and after World War I and played for Wales in the 1921 and 1922 seasons. He refereed the Scotland versus England water polo match played in Penarth in 1936 and went on to be a goal judge and timekeeper in the 1948 London Olympics.

In the latter half of the 20th century, the team's success started to wane, although things picked up again after they moved to the new facility that was opened in the 1980s. At that time, a proposal was made to demolish the old baths and replace them with a new apartment block. Luckily, local residents objected, and although the public cannot access the inside, the buildings remain for everyone to enjoy from the promenade.

Address Bridgeman Road, Penarth, Cardiff, CF64 3NS, www.penarthswpc.org.uk | **Getting there** Bus 88 or 305 to Penarth Pier; train to Penarth | **Hours** Viewable from the outside only | **Tip** The nearest Olympic-length swimming pool (50 metres) is the Cardiff International Pool and Gym, just over the Afon Elái (www.leisurecentre.com).

73 Panorama Stone

A compass of connection

The Panorama Stone on Cardiff Bay indicates the direction of several places with links to Cardiff or Wales. One of these is Patagonia. In the middle of the 19th century, Welsh speakers were being persecuted by the authorities. One example of this was the use of the Welsh Not – a length of wood that was hung around a child's neck if they dared to utter any words of Welsh while at school. Many considered this situation to be intolerable, and it led to massive migration across the Atlantic.

In 1865, the Argentinian government offered an area of land to Welsh settlers, with no apparent consideration given to the fact that it was already home to the indigenous Tehuelche people. Later that year, 150 Welsh people, including some from the Valleys, arrived to find it was not the land of milk and honey they had been promised. The area had suffered a prolonged drought, and when the rain came, it ran straight off the land and caused significant flooding, destroying some of the Welsh homes. Luckily, many were helped by the indigenous people, and the community overcame these early challenges.

The influence of those Welsh settlers can still be seen in Patagonia. There are several Welsh-inspired place names, including Puerto Madryn, where they landed – now a sizeable city. The region holds an annual Eisteddfod festival. And some schools are bilingual, taught in Spanish and Welsh, so the language continues to survive in Argentina. And here in Wales, it is no longer a source of persecution but one of pride.

The other places on the stone include cities that Cardiff is twinned with – Stuttgart, Nantes, Lugansk and Xiamen. Also, Lesotho, in recognition of the world's first country twinning in 1985, and Bergen, which supplied local mines with timber for pit props. Several places in Wales are also indicated, including Caernarfon, where the Prince of Wales was invested in 1969.

Address Stuart Street, Cardiff, CF10 5BZ | Getting there Train to Cardiff Bay; bus 1, 1A, 8 or X2 to Mermaid Quay | Hours Accessible 24 hours | Tip There are several places you can learn to speak Welsh in Cardiff, including Learn Welsh Cardiff (www.cardiff.ac.uk/welsh/courses).

74 Parc Cefn Onn

A wheelie wonderful woodland walk

Whether large or small, gardens are usually associated with houses. However, when Ernest Prosser bought some land in 1910 to build a family home, his priority was the garden. His son Cecil was suffering from tuberculosis, and he hoped that a garden would give him some respite. The first feature he created was a summerhouse with a swimming pond below it. We now know that cold-water swimming can help with many conditions, and Prosser believed it would help his son. The remains of a circular changing hut can still be found among the trees. Sadly, Cecil died just a few years later, and his father decided not to build the house after all.

Prosser was the manager of Rhymney Valley Railway, which ran along the eastern boundary of the garden. He used railway sleepers for the changing hut and spoil from tunnel excavations for the rockery. He planted vast numbers of flowering shrubs, which still give a good show in spring.

Giant gunnera leaves flank the rear of the pond, and exotic trees such as dawn redwood and grand fir are mixed in with natives. Rhododendrons, azaleas and Japanese maples reach to the sky beneath the arms of a tall oak tree. A stream runs through the site, and where the path reaches its highest point in the valley, the shrubs drip with lichens and mosses.

The council has owned the garden since 1944 and extended it south to create a country park with routes through onto Caerphilly Mountain. There is a wheelchair-accessible figure-of-eight path around the park, with a wide boardwalk leading up the valley side to a viewing platform above the pond and a picnic field. The council has two all-terrain trampers available to hire for one day a week, which can be used to explore the park. Ernest Prosser has left a real legacy with this garden, particularly now it is owned by the council and, therefore, open to the public.

Address Cherry Orchard Road, Cardiff, CF14 0UE, www.outdoorcardiff.com | **Getting there** Train to Lisvane & Thornhill; bus 86 to Lisvane Station | **Hours** Daily 7am–dusk | **Tip** More exotic trees can be seen in Blackweir Arboretum at the northern end of Bute Park.

75 Park House

A stylish introduction

When James McConnochie first moved to Cardiff, he worked for the architect William Burges' father and got to know the family. McConnochie was also a friend of the Marquess of Bute, and it is possible that he introduced William Burges to the Marquess, resulting in the lavish renovation and decoration of Cardiff Castle.

When McConnochie wanted to build a house on some land opposite Cathays Park, he also contracted Burges, a man he knew and trusted, to be the architect. In the design, Burges used Bath stone from England, pink granite from Scotland and Pennant sandstone from Wales, probably Caerphilly. The house was finished by the time McConnochie became mayor in 1879.

As you might expect, the interior is nowhere near as opulent as that of the castle, despite sharing an architect, even allowing for the fact that the original decorative paintwork, if completed as planned, has been painted over. However, the house has beautiful tile and parquet floors, elegant marble chimneypieces and decorative woodwork in mahogany, teak and painted deal (a softwood). The only apparent flaw in Burges' design is the staircase. It is clearly designed to impress, but it appears to be fitted the wrong way round – with its back to the front door. So, rather than visitors being wowed with a view across the hall and up the staircase, they are initially confronted with the underside of the steps. It seems that Burges learnt from his mistakes – this flaw was corrected in his own house in Kensington, which has a similar layout but a different approach to the entrance hall.

Park House, although handsome, does not stand out as being particularly unusual in style within Cardiff. There's a good reason for that – it is the building that many others were modelled on. Other architects picked up on Burges' Early French Gothic style and applied it to other houses and even chapels in the area.

Address 20 Park Place, Cardiff, CF10 3DQ | Getting there Train to Cardiff Queen Street or Cathays; several buses to Greyfriars Road | Hours Viewable from the outside only | Tip Park House is opposite Gorsedd Gardens, a great place for a picnic on a summer's day.

76_Penarth Pier

Standing strong since 1895

The Last Night of the Proms has become an institution in Britain, but of course, there had to be a 'first night' sometime in the past. Until 1895, classical music was something reserved for the upper echelons of society. The Proms, which started that year, were designed to bring classical music to the masses, as they still do. In the same year, the first car journey took place in Britain – in a French car. By the end of the year, there were around 20 automobiles on the roads. The speed limit was just four miles per hour, and each car had to have a person walking in front of it, waving a flag to warn other road users.

That was the year and the society in which Penarth Pier was first opened, and it has seen some significant changes in its time. The pier is one of only two on the South Wales coast and is a little shorter than its counterpart at Mumbles, as it would otherwise have obstructed the shipping channels heading to and from Cardiff Docks.

In 1931, the pier suffered from an enormous fire that razed the pavilion on the seaward end, as well as much of the decking. The pier was repaired, but the pavilion was not rebuilt. However, the distinctive Art Deco pavilion on the landward end remains.

Keeping the pier away from the shipping channel did not save it from being struck by ships on two separate occasions. One was a steamship that operated from the pier, but it was a Canadian merchant ship that caused the most damage. The captain lost control in a gale in 1947 and mangled or broke as many as 70 of the pier's supporting columns. It took two years for the repairs to be complete.

The pier has been extensively renovated in recent years, is free to enjoy, and is an exceptional place from which to watch the sun rise over the Bristol Channel. There are somewhat more cars on the road now, and the only flags you are likely to see are on bunting ruffling in the breeze.

Address The Esplanade, Penarth, Cardiff, CF64 3AU, +44 (0)1446 725236, pavilion@valeofglamorgan.gov.uk | **Getting there** Bus 88 or 305 to Penarth Pier; train to Penarth | **Hours** Accessible 24 hours | **Tip** When the tide is in, the slipway to the north of the pier is a popular place for swimmers to enter the water. Please be careful – the tides here are often strong.

77 Penn Family Filter

Before the tap ran clear

Once upon a time, in the days of old when dragons roamed the land, it was safe to drink the water found in streams, rivers and lakes. It probably still is in remote areas, high up the water catchment and away from human activity. However, as people started to congregate into larger groups, those water supplies quickly became contaminated with human and livestock waste, compounded over time with chemical waste.

It is not a coincidence that people started drinking beer, as the brewing process stops many harmful bacteria from developing. Or that we are told that tea absolutely must be made with freshly drawn and boiled water, as boiling kills most nasties. Of course, it helps that both also taste good!

Imagine what town water was like in Cardiff in Victorian times. The town was crowded, full of people and industry, with plenty of opportunities for the water to become contaminated both in the urban area and in the valleys further upstream. Cardiff's water was abstracted from the Glamorganshire Canal and the River Taff, which is where its sewage was also disposed of. Once the water filter was invented, families like the Penns from Grangetown could treat their own. This one was used by the Penns around the turn of the 20th century.

Contaminated water can lead to the spread of diseases such as cholera and dysentery. Diarrhoea may seem trivial, but it is not to be sniffed at – around one million people die from it worldwide every year. Although Cardiff's town water has been potable for some time, and water filters like this were available as long as 130 years ago, there are still over two million people worldwide who don't routinely have access to clean drinking water and suffer the consequences. Water filters using the same process are still being offered to people in need, as charities and other bodies work hard to make water poverty a thing of the past.

Address The Old Library, The Hayes, St David's Centre, Cardiff, CF10 1BH, +44 (0) 292 034 6214, www.cardiffmuseum.com, cardiffstory@cardiff.gov.uk | Getting there Bus 44, 45, 49 or 50 to Castle Street; train to Cardiff Central | Hours Mon–Sat 10am–4pm | Tip The Old Library is also home to a splendid Victorian corridor with a mosaic floor and patterned tiled walls.

78 Plasma Soup

Where lightning strikes twice

Have you ever wondered how hard it is to dock with the International Space Station? Or what those lines squiggling across maps mean? Have you ever wanted to (safely) feel the force of a hurricane or the unsettling power of an earthquake? Or make a ball roll uphill? Visiting Techniquest allows you to play with science and try out all of these things for yourself.

The mesmerising strands of electricity dancing a paso doble in the plasma ball are always popular. After all, you don't often get to control lightning! Plasma balls are filled with a very low-density gas such as neon, and this low density makes it easier to create an electrical discharge, which is exactly what these filaments of plasma are. A coil of wires in the middle of the ball is oscillating at such a high frequency that it heats up and the electrons are shaken off their atoms, forming an 'ionized gas', a soup of negatively charged electrons and positively charged ions. The electrons repel each other, forming these fingers of light to the edge of the glass. When you place your hand against the glass, the plasma arcs to your touch, because your body acts as a lightning rod, providing an easy route for the electrons to discharge to earth.

Although plasma balls could just be seen as novelty items, the principles behind them have practical applications. For example, plasma physics is used in fusion-energy research, where scientists aim to recreate the conditions inside stars to generate clean, abundant energy. Although visitors to Techniquest enjoy the hypnotic display in the plasma ball, this demonstrates that it is more than just a visual spectacle – it's a window into cutting-edge science and technology.

Whether you are young or old, interested in science, or just want to have some fun, Techniquest offers a thrilling place to spend a couple of hours down on Cardiff Bay.

Address Techniquest, Stuart Street, Cardiff, CF10 5BW, +44 (0) 292 047 5475, www.techniquest.org, info@techniquest.org | Getting there Train to Cardiff Bay (10-minute walk); Baycar 6 to Millennium Centre; bus 1, 8 or X2 to Mermaid Quay | Hours Daily (see website for times) | Tip If you need some sustenance after your visit, there are lots of cafés, bars and restaurants nearby. Walk straight ahead from the main entrance and you will soon find them.

79 Plasturton Gardens

A portal between worlds

As a centre of excellence for television filming, it is no surprise that Cardiff locations feature in several television series. One of these is the highly popular *His Dark Materials*, which was broadcast on BBC One between 2019 and 2022. Each of the three series covered one of the books in the trilogy written by Philip Pullman.

Some liken *His Dark Materials* to John Milton's poem *Paradise Lost*, which tells the story of the fall of humankind, based on his interpretation of the Book of Genesis. The name of the trilogy is indeed taken from a verse of *Paradise Lost*, and several theological themes run through the books. Indeed, some Christians consider the books to be blasphemous and unsuitable reading for their young-adult audience. However, when he was the Archbishop of Canterbury, Dr Rowan Williams suggested that the books would be an excellent stimulus for debate about the nature of Christianity.

In many quarters, the books have been well received. The first book in the trilogy, *Northern Lights*, won the Carnegie Medal for children's fiction, and the third book, *Amber Spyglass*, won the Whitbread Book of the Year award. A film of the trilogy starred Dakota Blue Richards, Nicole Kidman and Daniel Craig, amid a flurry of other stars. Called *The Golden Compass*, another reference to *Paradise Lost*, the film won an Oscar and a Bafta, but did not win over audiences and contributed to the demise of New Line Cinema.

In contrast, the BBC television version has been extremely popular. It won several awards, and audience appreciation rose with each series. Filmed at Wolf Studios near Cardiff Bay, several locations will be familiar to Cardiffians. One of these is the portal between the Oxford of Lyra's world, the world in which Will lives and the one that contains the city of Cittàgaze. For the eagle-eyed observer, those houses are not in Oxford, but Plasturton Gardens in Cardiff.

Address Plasturton Gardens, Pontcanna, Cardiff, CF11 9HF | Getting there Several buses to Beverley Hotel on Cathedral Road (3-minute walk) | Hours Accessible 24 hours | Tip Plasturton Gardens is not the only place in Cardiff that has been transposed with somewhere else. The National Museum of Wales has featured in several episodes of *Doctor Who*, once masquerading as the Musée d'Orsay in Paris.

80 Pneumoconiosis Mural

The fight for miners' lungs

A 1930s study revealed that 'miner's lung', which caused coughing, then shortness of breath, then severe breathing impairment and sometimes death, affected almost 100 times as many miners in South Wales as in England. After the conclusion of World War II, the coal-mining industry was seen as crucial to the country's recovery, and the government recognised the risk that this condition posed.

It is officially called 'pneumoconiosis' after the Greek for lung (pneumo) and dust (conios). The government established the Pneumoconiosis Research Unit at Llandough Hospital to understand the condition and reduce its incidence. When the unit X-rayed miners' lungs, they realised that the disease looked remarkably like silicosis, which was already known from mining silica. The trouble was that silicosis was often identified when the sufferer developed tuberculosis, but pneumoconiosis sufferers' disease did not develop similarly.

The researchers identified four levels of disease development that could be diagnosed by using X-rays. This allowed miners to be assessed before the disease started to impact their lives. Once the disease had reached level 2, they could be compensated and removed from mine working so it didn't develop further. The unit helped them to understand the sort of work they could do instead, boosting the morale of those affected.

That helped the mineworkers with the condition but did not reduce its incidence. There was something about the type of dust from Welsh coal that made Welsh miners more susceptible than those working in English coal mines. However, using water to reduce the amount of dust in the air was found to be highly effective, and these two interventions together led to the almost total elimination of the disease in the mining community.

Artist Michael Edmonds produced this mural in 1959 to commemorate the work of the unit.

Address University Hospital Llandough, Penlan Road, Llandough, Penarth, Cardiff, CF64 2XX | Getting there Bus 7, 95, 304 or 305 to Llandough Hospital; train to Cogan (25-minute walk) | Hours Accessible 24 hours | Tip Llandough Hospital is famous for the length of one of its corridors. Some accounts suggest it is a kilometre long, although the hospital itself states it is half that length.

81 Post Secrets

Peep show

Hundreds of thousands of shoppers will have walked past the artful bollards on The Hayes, blithely unaware that there is anything special about them. But for those who notice the slightly larger-than-usual posts, spot the decals that implore you to 'look inside' and follow those instructions, a treat is in store.

In the middle of the bustling thoroughfare in the heart of Cardiff's shopping district, the artist Jane Edden intended to create a moment of calm. As you peep through the spyhole in the bollards, a miniature scene comes into focus, static and monochrome, contrasting with the people hurrying past and the brightly coloured goods in the shop windows.

To meet the requirement for the art to be bilingual, the artist used body language, as it transcends the written word. She observed students at the Royal Welsh College of Music and Drama, and each post contains laser-cut figures from that study. The artist wants those who do peek inside to create their own stories around the vignettes. What are the subjects doing or thinking, and why? What directions have their lives taken? Are any of them now well known and well loved on the stage or screen?

The restrictive nature of the setting meant there were some technical challenges to overcome. Bollards are small and provide a confined space for anything placed inside them. These bollards are larger than average, but the work still had to be tiny to fit. The clever use of mirrors makes the art seem larger than it actually is, giving it a magical, TARDIS-like quality. Consideration had to be given to how the light changes during the day and seasons and how to manage condensation – the metal bollards are not protected from either the heat of the sun or the cold of winter.

There are 11 artful bollards containing 'Post Secrets' artwork. How many can you find, and what stories do they inspire in you?

Address The Hayes, St David's Centre, Cardiff, CF10 1AH | **Getting there** Several buses to city centre stops; train to Cardiff Central | **Hours** Accessible 24 hours | **Tip** For contemporary art for your home, head to gallery TEN. in Roath (www.gallery-ten.co.uk).

82 Postbox Subsumed by a Tree

Special delivery

Trees are the most amazing organisms: we spend enormous amounts of money trying to engineer methods of sequestering carbon dioxide to combat climate change, yet, it is something that trees do effortlessly, naturally and effectively, and at no cost to us. Trees supply us with timber and provide us – and many other animals on Earth – with food and shelter, playing an essential role in the web of life.

Silver birches trap particulate pollution in their leaves and drop it to the ground every autumn rather than allowing it to block our lungs. London plane trees do similar, but with their bark. Trees even communicate with each other underground and through the air.

We love gazing up through the branches of trees to glimpse a blue sky, walking in their cool shade on a hot summer's day, and kicking through their leaves in autumn. Trees release volatile organic compounds that improve our mood, and oxygen that allows us to live.

We also imagine all sorts of horrors associated with trees: trees that rebel and whomp us if we get too close and others that wind their roots around us if we stay still for too long. Both examples might be based on reality. After all, trees can destroy houses, cars and people if we get too close during a storm. And trees will subsume things that get in their way. There are several examples of a bicycle that has been propped up against a tree and left – and then found several metres in the air after the tree has grown around it and up.

This postbox is a good example – the tree continues to grow regardless of the lump of red steel placed in its way. The Royal Mail has stopped collections from it because they deem it too dangerous (do the posties really stand still for that long?), but the tree is loved, so it will stay, and the postbox is being sacrificed to its need for space.

Address Morlais Street, Cardiff, CF23 5EP | **Getting there** Bus 28 or 29 to Tydfil Place | **Hours** Accessible 24 hours | **Tip** Opposite the postbox, Roath Pleasure Gardens have a beautiful display of cherry blossom in spring.

83 Principality Building Society HQ

A mutual understanding

Building societies are 'mutuals': they act on behalf of their members, not shareholders. With early building societies, each member made regular payments, and when there was enough money available, one would receive a payout large enough to buy a plot of land and build a home. Everyone continued with their payments until the final member had received their payout, at which point the building society was terminated. This model has been superseded by 'permanent' societies, in which members can save for something special or borrow for a home, and each balances the other out.

In the 1980s, the government passed legislation that allowed building societies to demutualise and become banks, which many took advantage of. However, the trend is beginning to reverse as many people see mutual financial institutions as more beneficial.

The Principality Building Society was formed as a permanent society in 1860 and has served the people of Wales ever since. These headquarters were built in 1914. The building society has grown to have over 500,000 members, all of whom can have a say in how the society is run. With no shareholders to please, the society supports local communities instead, focusing on young people and providing financial education. It has committed to net-zero carbon emissions and made significant inroads towards that target, also supporting developers to build energy-efficient homes. Staff are valued just as much as customers, with engagement, personal and professional development, and support programmes in place.

Over a century after its establishment, the Principality Building Society continues to be headquartered nearby and operates a branch from this impressive building in the centre of the city.

Address Queen Street, Cardiff, CF10 2PB, www.principality.co.uk | Getting there Several buses to Kingsway or Castle stops; train to Cardiff Central or Cathays | Hours Viewable from the outside only | Tip When it's time to escape the hubbub of Queen Street, Exitus Escape Rooms might be just what you're looking for (90A Queen Street, www.exitusescaperoomscardiff.co.uk).

84 The Pumping Station

Engineering a healthier city

How frequently do you think about what happens to human sewage? It's not something that we need to consider very often these days. However, in the mid-1800s, things looked – and smelt – very different in Cardiff. Many houses did not even have a privy, and 'night soil' was tipped into the quay or onto the streets. Even the drinking water was often contaminated with sewage, which leaked from nearby cesspits or was dumped into the same rivers that drinking water was extracted from.

After the cholera epidemic of 1849, when over 300 people in Cardiff died, the provision of clean water moved up the political agenda. A privately owned company was set up by legal statute to provide clean drinking water in Cardiff, and work was done to improve the provision of toilet facilities, drainage and sewage removal. The project was successful, and over the next 50 years, the death rate halved. Removing sewage required the use of pumps, as gravity would not be sufficient alone. When this pumping station was opened in 1910, the pumps were still powered by enormous steam engines, which is why it is such a cavernous building.

Across the UK, water and sewage pumping stations were seen as civic buildings and therefore designed to look grand as well as being functional. This is a fine example of such a building. However, when electric pumps came into use, it was no longer necessary to operate from such a large site. The Pumping Station is now an antiques centre with several traders throughout the space. The old footings for the steam engines are still visible on the ground.

Cardiff's sewage is now pumped to a modern plant at Tremorfa, where non-degradable solids such as wipes, nappies and other things that should not be flushed down toilets are removed, and the sewage is treated. Local farms use the remaining solids as fertiliser, and the cleaned liquid is released into the estuary.

Address Penarth Road, Cardiff, CF11 8TT | Getting there Bus 92, 93 or 94 to Brindley Road; train to Grangetown (Cardiff) and a 20-minute walk | Hours Viewable from outside 24 hours; see website for opening hours | Tip The Pumping Station was built by the engineer William Harper. He is responsible for many other civic structures in Cardiff, including the water tower on Cyncoed Road that was once a pumping station for the nearby reservoir (no longer there). The tower remains a local landmark, although it is now part of a private residence.

85_The Queens Vaults

Where ships once moored

Westgate Street, which runs from the castle to Cardiff Central railway station, arcs gracefully as it passes what was the medieval city. Most other streets in the Old Town are pretty straight, so why does this one buck the trend?

Built on the banks of the River Taff close to the sea, Cardiff was plagued by flooding, particularly during periods of heavy rain combined with spring tides. When the South Wales Railway was being built in the middle of the 19th century, Cardiff Corporation and Lord Bute saw an opportunity to improve this situation. They asked Isambard Kingdom Brunel, who was building the railway, to divert the flow to take a new course due south from Cardiff Bridge. This would move the river further from the town, reduce erosion on the town side of its bend and increase the rate of flow into the sea. It created an area of reclaimed land big enough to house the new railway station and enlarge Cardiff Arms Park. The tactic worked, and flooding has been much reduced.

In the middle of the previous century, the river had begun to silt up, so taxes were levied to pay for the maintenance of the waterway and quay. This was enough to keep the quay in operation for a while, but the size of ships that could be accommodated had shrunk, and new docks for larger vessels were being built south of the town. The quay's importance diminished, and once the river was diverted, it was closed.

It took some years after the river was moved before the Corporation infilled its cut. At that point, a new street was built along the river's old course. Initially, this was called Park Road, but has since been renamed Westgate Street. The graceful curve of the street reflects the original route of the river. The Queens Vaults is a Victorian pub that was built on the old quayside at about the time the road was constructed, and has been serving thirsty customers ever since.

Address 29 Westgate Street, Cardiff, CF10 1EH | **Getting there** Several buses to Westgate Street; train to Cardiff Central | **Hours** Fri & Sat 10am–1am, Sun–Thu 10am–midnight | **Tip** A little further up Westgate Street by the stadium entrance is a red and black brick building with a balcony below its roof. This was built in 1878 as a racquets and fives club after the old river course was filled in. It is now the Welsh Rugby Union shop.

86 Radyr Hydro Scheme

From emergency declaration to energy generation

Cardiff is planning to be a One Planet City by 2050. The city council has recognised that we are living in a climate emergency and is committed to taking responsibility for its part in achieving the goals of the Paris Agreement climate-change treaty. The strategy is designed to enable the city to become carbon neutral, support a growing green economy and improve residents' wellbeing.

Some projects have already been implemented. These include the construction of a large solar farm on Lamby Way, which provides renewable power to the nearby wastewater treatment plant and feeds electricity into the grid.

There has been a weir here for over a century, as some of the water used to be diverted via a small canal to power the Melingriffith Tin Works a little further downstream. Almost 70 years after the tin works closed, the water is again being used to generate electricity. This time, two large Archimedes' screws make the most of the head of water created by the weir. Each turbine is four metres wide and ten metres long, and both are visible from the riverbank below. As the water passes down through the screws, they turn and generate electricity. In the first year of operation, this power station generated around 1 million kWh of renewable electricity – enough to power around 250 semi-detached homes.

The next project to go live will be a network that provides waste heat from one of the city's incinerators to the buildings in the Cardiff Bay and Butetown areas. This is ultimately expected to reduce carbon emissions by around 4,000 tonnes a year. Other projects the city is implementing include improving the energy efficiency of buildings, encouraging active transport and providing electric-vehicle chargers, reducing the carbon impact of procurement, increasing opportunities to recycle waste, encouraging food growing in the city and expanding the city's tree canopy.

Address Longwood Drive, Cardiff, CF15 8AA, www.cardiff.gov.uk | Getting there Bus 63 to Station Road or King's Road (15-minute walk); train to Radyr (11-minute walk) | Hours Viewable from the outside only | Tip Growing your own is a fun and tasty way to reduce your carbon footprint. Cardiff has 28 allotment sites, including Forest Farm Allotments about a kilometre downstream of the weir (www.outdoorcardiff.com/allotments).

87 Rhiwbina Garden Village

A working-class idyll?

The Industrial Revolution created many benefits, particularly for landowners and those in the middle classes. It did generate jobs for working-class people, but it also led to many living in poor-quality accommodation and slums. In response to this situation, Ebenezer Howard promoted an alternative way to grow a city. He proposed encircling the urban area with a greenbelt that would provide food for residents and house other essential services such as reservoirs and health facilities. Beyond this greenbelt, other small cities, surrounded by their own greenbelts and associated services, would be connected to each other and the central city by train and canal. Everyone would have access to good-quality housing, greenspace and work, and everything would be cooperatively owned, thus ending the exploitation of tenants.

Howard's books were so popular that he decided to try to implement his idea. However, he ran into trouble trying to sell the concept to existing working-class cooperatives. As a result, to get one of these new-style cities built, he had to go to private investors. The result was Letchworth Garden City, which was an instant hit. House prices rose, the investors received their dividends, and the benefits were felt by the middle classes – not what he had intended.

Although only two garden cities were ever built in the UK, the concept was developed further to create several 'New Towns', and has become popular in other parts of the world. On a smaller scale, 189 houses were built around World War I to create Rhiwbena Garden Village. They were cooperatively owned, and rents were charged at cost. Unfortunately, the loan used to build the houses needed to be repaid after World War II, resulting in the homes being sold to their tenants in 1968.

Rhiwbina Garden Village is now a desirable, leafy, middle-class suburb of Cardiff, with house prices to match.

Address Lon-Y-Dail, Cardiff, CF14 6DZ | Getting there Train to Rhiwbina; bus 21 or 23 to Rhiwbina | Hours Houses viewable from the outside only | Tip Poet, author and first curator of St Fagans National Museum of History, Iorwerth Cyfeiliog Peate, lived at 29 Lon-Y-Dail, where a blue plaque hangs above the door.

88 Riverside Market

A feast for the senses

Thanks to its status as a busy international port, Cardiff has long been a multicultural city. This is reflected in the artisan food stalls in the weekly Riverside Market. Alongside traditional British pastries and Welsh cakes, you will find specialities made in Cardiff that originate in Portugal, Brazil and Greece. The street food on offer makes this an experience rather than just shopping. It is similarly multicultural, featuring Italian, Sichuan and Middle Eastern delicacies. And of course, it wouldn't be a market in the 21st century without offering wood-fired pizza as well.

The primary focus of the market, however, is on locally grown and produced food, some of which is organic. Tables are piled high with basics such as eggs, butter and cheese, and boxes of organic fruits and vegetables. As this is locally grown food, the offerings change with the seasons, from succulent Welsh berries and salads in the summer to hearty root vegetables in the winter. Alongside these are stalls that sell game, speciality meat from rare and traditional breeds, and cuts of organically raised meat. Check the market's website to see who the stallholders are and what they are offering this week.

This variety means the air is filled with the mouthwatering fragrances of fresh coffee, freshly baked bread and sizzling street food. The market throngs with shoppers from across the city enjoying the opportunity to meet the people who produce their food and chat to friends over a spot of lunch.

The market has been running since 2009, growing from just a handful of stalls to become one of Wales' most celebrated food destinations. Its setting along the banks of the River Taff, near the castle and overlooked by the Principality Stadium, makes it easy for anyone in Cardiff or its environs to access. This is a must-visit place for all Cardiffian foodies.

Address Fitzhamon Embankment, Cardiff, CF11 6AN, www.riversidemarket.org.uk, booking@cardifffarmersmarkets.org.uk | Getting there Bus 44, 45, 49 or 50 to Castle Street; train to Cardiff Central | Hours Sun 10am–2pm | Tip The same people hold farmers' markets in Roath on Saturdays, Rhiwbina on Fridays and Cardiff Met during term time.

89_Roath Lock Drama Village

Doctor Who?

Who would have thought that a modern building with such an unusual façade would be the home of the BBC's longest-running television soap opera? Pobol y Cwm, a Welsh-language show, has been broadcast several times a week for over 50 years, although not always from this building. Within the confines of the Roath Lock Drama Village lies the outdoor Cwmderi High Street, as well as the indoor sets such as the school and pub.

For 10 years, this building was also home to *Doctor Who*, and nine of the Doctors were filmed here. Unfortunately, you are unlikely to bump into any of them entering or leaving these days, as the filming has now moved to Wolf Studios Wales on Glass Avenue. However, you may bump into other familiar doctors (or nurses), as *Casualty* is also filmed here. You might see them in a local hospital, too, as actors shadow real Accident and Emergency staff to prepare for their on-screen roles. Despite airing weekly, each episode takes two weeks to film, so more than one is in progress simultaneously.

Roath Lock Drama Village is not only the home of outstanding television production; it is also the home of outstanding sustainable architecture. When the building was opened in 2012, it was the largest in Wales to have achieved the BREEAM Outstanding sustainable-construction certification. One of its features is the use of rainwater collected from the roof to flush the toilets, and it also uses low-energy technology for most of its lighting. In addition, the corporation has a highly regarded apprenticeship scheme, offering young people entry into the creative world without building up student debt.

The façade does a great job of hiding what is essentially a massive box. It is simply a series of clip-on timber panels that create this 300-metre-long, other-worldly, somewhat surreal effect; without it, the building would look like a big shed.

Address BBC Roath Lock Drama Village, Porth Teigr Way, Cardiff, CF10 4GA | Getting there Skycar bus to Porth Teigr Way; train or tram to Cardiff Bay (20-minute walk); on-street parking (it gets crowded) | Hours Viewable from the outside only | Tip There are also BBC studios on Central Square, which offer tours (www.bbc.co.uk/showsandtours/tours/bbc-cymru-wales-central-square-cardiff).

90 Roath Mill

Medieval Cardiff's breadbasket

After the Normans arrived in Cardiff and built their castle, the burgeoning population needed to be fed. Although some houses within the town walls had gardens in which they could grow fruits and vegetables, space was required outside the urban area for grazing and cereals. The land chosen for this purpose was around Roath.

In the next couple of centuries, Roath's farming area rose to 305 acres of arable land that was used to grow crops, including cereals such as wheat, rye, barley and oats. One hundred acres were set to pasture, and a further 102 for growing hay, which was used as animal feed. A significant quantity of butter and cheese was produced here, so some of the grazing was used by cows. There were at least two mills operating in the area. One was a fulling mill, suggesting that sheep as well as cattle grazed locally – fulling is a process whereby a woollen fabric is cleaned and then pounded to felt it. The result is a versatile material that is warm and water-resistant. Another word for fulling is tucking, and those who made their living from this activity were given the surname of Fuller or Tucker.

Roath Mill as modelled was first documented in 1102 but may have been older, and milled grain. Over the millennium during which it is thought to have been used, the building would have been reconstructed several times. The last building was still in use close to the end of the 19th century, by which point waterpower had largely been replaced by steam. Little of the structure has survived, although if you look closely, you may be able to spot the remains of a wall next to the stream.

In 1910, the land around the stream was given to the Cardiff Corporation by the Tredegar Estate, which was developing the area. When the council created the park, they used waste to create the levels, which probably included any stone that remained from the mill.

Address Sandringham Road, Cardiff, CF23 5BL | **Getting there** Bus 1, 1A or 2 to Waterloo Gardens; on-street parking nearby | **Hours** Accessible 24 hours | **Tip** Poet and writer Dannie Abse lived at 66 Sandringham Road, where a blue plaque hangs on the front wall.

91 Roman Gods

Classical confusion

The Grade I-listed Glamorgan building in Cathays Park is flanked by two impressive statues, each featuring a Roman God. These represent Cardiff's two primary sources of wealth, namely mining and navigation.

On the left, mining is represented by three men straining to move heavy loads of stone, even though mining for *coal* rather than stone brought prosperity to South Wales. With them are two women, one of whom is Minerva, the Roman goddess of war, wisdom and handicrafts, who is wearing a helmet and carrying a shield. Despite her name, which includes the letters 'mine' but derives from old words for intelligence, there is no apparent connection to mining of coal or anything else.

The connection to the god in the statue on the right is more apparent. Navigation is represented by a man and woman riding on a boat being drawn at speed by a pair of mythological creatures that are part horse and part fish, known as hippocampi. Another man is not in the boat, but gripping the neck of one of these creatures and being dragged along in the water. Hippocampi are often associated with Neptune, the Roman god of the sea, so the link to the port and navigation is clear.

If these statues look and sound similar to those of Greek mythology, that's no coincidence. As Romans conquered new lands, they assimilated many customs, myths and beliefs into their own. The Romans adopted every Greek god and goddess, so Minerva and Neptune started life as Athena and Poseidon.

Both statues have one figure who is unlikely to be noticed from the front – it is worth walking around the back of each to appreciate them fully. Although these statues are in a classical style, they are relatively modern, having been created around the turn of the 20th century when the Glamorgan Building was constructed. The sculptor was Albert Hodge, a Scot whose work can be seen in several places around the UK.

Address King Edward VII Avenue, Cardiff, CF10 3ND | **Getting there** Several buses to Greyfriars Road Stop GN, Kingsway Hilton Stop GP or Law Courts Stop RJ; train to Cathays | **Hours** Accessible 24 hours | **Tip** For a rather less classical sculpture, head to the barrage, where you will find Roald Dahl's *The Enormous Crocodile* (www.cardiffharbour.com).

92 Rugby Codebreakers

Sporting giants

On several occasions in the last half a century, there have been attempts to set up a professional Rugby League team in Cardiff. However, they have all faltered and failed after a short time. This city is dedicated to Rugby Union and has little interest in switching allegiances to the other code.

Despite that, Cardiff has produced an array of rugby players who have defected to Rugby League, either to avoid the racism they encountered in Rugby Union or just so they could become professionals – Rugby Union did not become a professional sport until 1995. And some of these Cardiffian codebreakers grew to become giants in the game.

The 13 players listed on this statue were all born between 1879 and 1960 in Tiger Bay, Butetown, Grangetown, Adamsdown and Splott. As you would expect from a multicultural community, they represent a variety of ethnic origins. This group has three Rugby League World Cup winners, three Rugby League Hall of Famers, four on the Welsh Sports Hall of Fame Roll of Honour and seven winners of a Challenge Cup final. Nine were Great Britain internationals, and 12 were Welsh internationals. Among their number is the first Black player to represent Great Britain, the first black coach in professional sport in the UK and the first Black captain of a Great Britain team. All played professionally in the north of England because they couldn't do so in Wales.

Cardiff has a rich history of erecting statues of white men. The first statue of a real, named Welsh woman in Wales was erected in Cardiff as late as 2021, and it took until 2023 to unveil this statue – the first of a real, named Black man in the whole of Wales.

Hopefully, the racism that dogged many of these players will soon be erased from the sport – and across society – and Wales will see more celebration of the complete variety of our cultural heritage.

Address Stuart Place, Cardiff, CF10 5BZ, www.rugbycodebreakers.co.uk | Getting there Train to Cardiff Bay; bus 1, 1A, 8 or X2 to Mermaid Quay | Hours Accessible 24 hours | Tip CoffiCo Mermaid Quay has a coffee shop on a pier that gives a view of the statue from a different angle (www.coffico.uk).

93 Sauropodomorpha Footprints

Penarth's prehistoric pedestrians

African bull elephants are Earth's largest land animal. They are enormous – usually about 3 metres high to their shoulders, and 6 tonnes in weight. So imagine a land animal weighing as much as 60 tonnes – 10 times as much as an African bull elephant. Morph that body into something resembling a gigantic lizard, and you have an idea of what a sauropodomorpha dinosaur was like. Its long neck enabled it to reach higher leaves than the other dinosaurs of its time, and its long heavy tail counterbalanced the weight of its head and neck as it reached out.

These are the largest terrestrial animals ever, and they lived in South Wales over 200 million years ago, in the Late Triassic period. It wasn't South Wales then, of course. And no humans ever saw one of these beasts alive – it was another 195 million years before any of our evolutionary ancestors turned up on the scene.

The Bristol Channel is one of the best places in the UK for evidence of Late Triassic terrestrial tetrapods. (Tetrapods have four limbs, but if they walk on two of their four limbs, they are not quadrupeds but bipeds.) It was not until 2009 that academics noticed and started documenting these footprints at the bottom of the cliffs near Penarth. Several tracks, some overlapping, can be seen for about 50 metres. The prints are all circular or elliptical and are surrounded by displacement rings where the mud squelched out from underneath the dinosaurs' feet. The prints range from 20 to 60 centimetres in diameter and are 5 to 10 centimetres deep.

Since a fossil of a sauropod was found on the far side of the Bristol Channel, that is what academics think these footprints belonged to. Since they were first studied in 2009, the footprints have already been noticeably eroded, so if you want to see them, the sooner, the better.

Address Penarth Beach, Cardiff, CF64 3AU | Getting there Bus 88 or 305 to Penarth Pier; train to Penarth; walk 830 metres south along the beach from the bottom of Cliff Hill; position accurately marked on Google Maps | Hours Daylight hours, not accessible at high tide; check tide times before visiting | Tip You can pick up a guide to finding the footprints and other items to support the valuable work of the RNLI at the shop in the lifeboat station at Penarth (www.rnli.org).

94 Scale the Stadium

A bird's-eye view

Where can you stand in Cardiff and see the pitch on which the Wales women's rugby team won the Six Nations in 2024, Llandaff Cathedral, the Pierhead building, the Cardiff Bay Barrage and the radio mast on Flat Holm Island? It might seem impossible… until you consider where you might get a bird's-eye view.

The tour of the stadium roof begins sedately with a health and safety briefing. Next is the energetic bit – climbing up 15 flights of stairs to get there. Clipping into the safety rails and enjoying the first view gives you a chance to recover your breath. Your heart might continue thumping, though, as you walk along the edge of the roof and up the middle of the arch to the very top.

This is where that view is. If the roof is closed, you can see into the castle. If it is open, you can see down into the stadium instead. Either way, it is a fabulous viewing point, and your guide will talk you through what you can see.

The fun doesn't end there, though. Back down to the edge of the stadium, it is time to walk across the Spire – a platform built out over the river, 35 metres above water level. Although you are clipped in, and therefore perfectly safe, there is no rail between you and the drop. Whatever your brain says about safety, your heart is sure to tell you something else!

If you book the zip, the next experience involves another climb – this time up steep steps to the 'Crow's Nest', which is 60 metres above pitch level. A zipwire will then whisk you back to the roof, along the length of the stadium (sadly, not across the pitch).

And then there is the question of getting back down to ground level. There are two ways to tackle this – the slow way, back down the stairs, or the fast way. More clipping in, and then a step over nothing to face the stadium. Heart thumping, walk a few paces down the wall, and then… swing and drop!

Address Westgate Street, Cardiff, CF10 1NS, https://bookings.principalitystadium.wales/stadiumtours/scale.htm | Getting there Several buses to Cardiff Bridge; train to Cardiff Central | Hours Open for scheduled tours only; reservation required | Tip For more high-level thrills, there are several climbing walls in Cardiff, including Fun HQ at the International Sports Village, which also has a drop slide (www.funhqcardiff.co.uk).

95 Scott Memorial

The lighthouse in the lake

The urge to explore seems to be something innate in the human race. As children, it may start in a garden, local park or woodland. For many, the urge continues and explains the popularity of foreign and adventure holidays. For some, it goes even further; it is frontiers they want to explore, and they will risk their lives to do so.

This was the case for Captain Scott and his team as they left Cardiff in 1910 with the South Pole in their sights. The expedition is most remembered for its failures and the demise of five of the team, including Captain Scott. However, their ambition was still celebrated when the ship returned. The quaysides were lined with crowds to watch the *Terra Nova* sail back into dock in 1913, and when the ship's owner, Mr Bowring, gave the city its figurehead, it was proudly placed alongside the promenade in Roath Park for visitors to admire. At the figurehead's presentation ceremony, Mr Bowring announced his intention to also donate a clock tower to honour Scott and his expedition.

This clock tower, in the form of a lighthouse, has become one of the iconic landmarks of Cardiff. Finished in 1915, the clock had to be wound weekly for more than 50 years. This was done by hand, by climbing a ladder inside the tower. In the 1970s, it was not considered a good use of taxpayer funds to employ someone for that, and an electrical mechanism was added. This also enabled the lighthouse to be lit for the first time, illuminating the clock faces.

A small veranda on the third level can fit several people – as long as they can contort themselves through a tiny doorway at the top of the ladder! You won't see the figurehead in the park any longer – it was deemed too valuable to leave exposed to the elements, and it is now looked after by the National Museum of Wales.

Which frontier will the next adventurers with links to Cardiff explore? Only time will tell.

Address Lake Road, Cardiff, CF23 5PH | Getting there Bus 28 or 29 to Promenade East; train to Heath Low Level or Heath High Level | Hours Daily 7.30am–dusk | Tip At the western end of the promenade, Terra Nova Café is a popular place for pizzas and afternoon teas (+44 (0) 292 076 4370).

96 Senedd

Transparent democracy

The Senedd building is one of a kind, as it was designed to enhance collaborative democracy in a country with sustainability as a core value. Some other democratic institutions, such as the Houses of Parliament, encourage a combative style of politics, with the government and opposition facing each other, ready to shout each other down. Here, though, the Siambr (debating chamber) is circular. Modern technology allows members to raise their hands to speak and discuss issues within their own party via computers rather than whispering or sending notes along benches. The building and its rooms were given glass sides and viewing balconies to represent transparency in the democratic process.

The design is both striking and functional. The vast mass of concrete and slate absorbs and releases heat slowly, keeping the temperature more stable than in many modern buildings. The funnel above the Siambr leads to a cowl that turns in the breeze. As wind passes over it, it creates a vacuum that draws hot air up and out of the building. Vents in the floor replace that hot air with cool. The same funnel acts as a light well. Although clad with cedar on the outside, it has aluminium rings on the inside. These reflect and diffuse the light, improving its quality for those working in the Siambr below. Boreholes bring warmth from the ground in winter and coolness in the summer, and a biomass boiler is used for any additional heating needed over the winter months.

Even water use has been considered, with rain collected from the roof used to flush the toilets. The building has achieved excellence in sustainability and reminds the government of its aim to do the same.

In the 20th century, Cardiff became a city (1905), Wales' first-ever capital city (1955), and the home of the first Welsh parliament (1999). In the 21st century, what exciting future awaits?

Address Pierhead Street, Cardiff, CF99 1SN, www.senedd.wales | Getting there Train to Cardiff Bay; bus 1, 1A, 8 or X2 to Mermaid Quay | Hours See website for current information on visiting | Tip Cardiff's City Hall, opened in 1904, is a more traditional building, built from stone and designed to impress according to Edwardian values (Cathays Park, CF10 3ND).

97 Shand House

A visionary's legacy

When Frances Batty Shand was born to a plantation-owning father and enslaved mother in Jamaica, few would have predicted what a visionary she would become. At the tender age of four, she was sent away from home to Scotland, where she probably stayed with her father's family. Around the middle of the 19th century, she moved to Cardiff to be near her brother, who was working for Rhymney Railway Company.

Frances witnessed much squalor and hardship as well as opportunity in the rapidly growing town, and her initial concern was for the children who were wearing rags and living in terrible conditions. Her focus then moved to people with sight loss. At that time, there was no welfare state and no national charity to support blind people, and it was difficult for people with impaired vision to find employment. She got to work and set up a charity that became the Cardiff Institute for the Blind, now known as Sight Life. The institute initially employed five blind men in a basket-weaving workshop. Frances' brother died 12 years after she founded the charity, and she moved away. However, she left the charity in good hands, and it thrived. By 1900, it employed 100 blind people, making a variety of products needed in a busy port. By 2006, the charity provided other types of support, and the workshop was closed as it was no longer needed.

Around 2.5 per cent of people who live in Cardiff have sight loss, and 1,500 are registered blind or partially sighted. Consideration of people with sight loss is not always at the forefront of decision making, so the charity is needed as much now as ever.

The initial workshop building was destroyed in an air raid during World War II, and Shand House was built to replace it. Sight Life has moved premises, but the building retains its name in honour of the founder of a charity that has been an important part of Cardiff society for over 150 years.

Address 20 Newport Road, Cardiff, CF24 0DB, www.sightlife.wales | **Getting there** Several buses to Fitzalan Place or West Grove; train to Cardiff Queen Street | **Hours** Viewable from the outside only | **Tip** If you are a disabled person in Cardiff looking for sporting opportunities, Met Community may be able to help you find a club (www.sportcardiff.co.uk/disability-sport).

98 Sisley's Tree

Making a good impression

Impressionism emerged in Paris in the 1870s as a radical departure from the style and subject matter of traditional French paintings. Photography was beginning to take hold as an art form and compete directly with the style of conventional French paintings, which produced images that were as realistic as possible.

Alfred Sisley met Monet, Renoir and Bazille while studying. They found that they shared an interest in painting landscapes and focusing on how light changed perception. They left their brush strokes visible and used bright and bold colours, painting their feelings rather than the detail of what they saw. This new style of painting was dazzling, radical and broadly disliked by critics and the public. The name of the movement came from a satirical review of Monet's painting *Impression, Soleil Levant – Impression, Sunrise.* However, as with many ideas, it grew on the public and slowly gained in popularity.

Sisley was the only leading Impressionist to paint in Wales. Although he was British by nationality, he lived in France his entire life. He and his long-term partner Eugenie had two children, and when they both found themselves in failing health, they decided it would be a good time to marry. They completed the formalities at Cardiff Register Office and stayed in Penarth and Langland for several months.

We know of six paintings from his stay in Penarth. He loved watching the ships sailing to and from the port, and one of his paintings depicts a mother and daughter on the clifftops watching a paddle steamer approach Penarth Pier. The painting depicts two trees, one of which was still standing a century later. However, it met its end early in the 21st century due to clifftop erosion. The present oak tree was planted further inland to replace the one that was lost and keep the memory of Sisley's visit to Cardiff and Penarth alive.

Address Cliff Hill, Penarth, Cardiff, CF64 5BP | **Getting there** Bus 88 or 305 to Cliff Walk or Alberta Road; train to Penarth (16-minute walk); parking at Cliff Parade, CF64 5BP | **Hours** Accessible 24 hours | **Tip** Around 200 metres to the south of the tree, next to Penarth Cliff Top Park and the car park, there are two popular cafés: Willmores 1938 and Cioni Bistro (www.facebook.com/willmores1938, www.cionis.co.uk).

99 Snoop Dogg's Classroom

A lesson in growing giant vegetables

If someone talks about a grandpa growing vegetables, the image conjured might be that of a man in tweeds on his allotment. Perhaps not, when that grandpa is Snoop Dogg, the hip-hop star who is known for his marijuana consumption.

Calvin Broadus Jr's mum thought he looked like the Peanuts character Snoopy when he was a child, hence the 'Snoop' moniker. Snoop Dogg has courted controversy since his middle-school years, when he caused a commotion by rapping in the corridors. His musical career skyrocketed from the moment his first album, *Doggystyle*, was released, but he also embraced a gangster lifestyle. It seems that violence was an everyday part of life, and he was once charged with murdering a rival gang member, for which he was eventually acquitted. Having lost several friends and family members to gang-related violence, he decided to change direction and head towards the mainstream.

So mainstream, in fact, that he even starred in a cookery series alongside Martha Stewart – *Martha & Snoop's Potluck Dinner Party*. Perhaps this interest in food was developed as a result of meeting Ian Neale in Cardiff. When Snoop Dogg heard that Ian had grown the world's largest swede, he invited him to Utilita Arena for a backstage chat to share the secrets of his success. Snoop Dogg filmed his invitation in front of an image of a field of marijuana, so there was little doubt about which 'vegetables' he was referring to.

More recently, he was a torch-bearer and commentator at the 2024 Paris Olympics and became a coach on *The Voice* talent show. His role at the Olympics continued his unexpected career evolution, which has included acting, investing (including in several cannabis-related businesses) and product endorsements. The controversy has not ended, but neither has his talent, and record sales keep racking up, possibly even more than the size of one of Ian Neale's swedes.

Address Mary Ann Street, Cardiff, CF10 2EQ, +44 (0) 292 022 4488, www.utilitaarenacardiff.co.uk | **Getting there** Several buses to Lower Churchill Way or Bute Terrace; train to Cardiff Queen Street or Cardiff Central | **Hours** Viewable from the outside only, unless attending an event | **Tip** If you prefer smaller venues, Clwb Ifor Bach on Womanby Street hosts several gigs every week (www.clwb.net).

100_St Mary's Church

A ghostly outline

A contemporary illustration of the Great Flood of 1607 shows people clinging onto trees, a church submerged to the level of its gutters, and someone sitting on the roof of a building. Others are floating in the water with sheep, cattle and a baby in its crib. Eyewitnesses described 'huge and mighty hills of water' moving 'faster than a greyhound can run'. It suggests that, like a tsunami, the wave travelled so fast that it could not be outrun. It certainly killed a great many people.

The cause of the wave is disputed in academic circles. Some records of the event refer to stormy weather, yet others make no mention of the weather. Many believe the wave was caused by an unusually high spring tide, low atmospheric pressure that increased its height and hurricane-force winds that pushed an even greater volume of water up the Bristol Channel. An alternative theory is that the wave was caused by an earthquake along the fault line that lies off southwest Ireland. Undersea earthquakes cause waves through the entire depth of the ocean, known as tsunamis. As tsunamis approach the shore, they slow. The wavelength shortens, the height of each wave grows and the force of the water increases.

Whether a tsunami or a storm surge caused the flood, it would have been amplified by the shape of the Bristol Channel, funnelling water towards the mouth of the River Severn.

Records suggest that the Great Flood significantly damaged St Mary's Church, which stood on the east bank of the River Taff, on the seaward side of Cardiff. A map drawn three years later shows that the river had encroached on the graveyard, but the tower was still standing. By 1678, the tower had collapsed, and the church had no roof. Although nothing remains of the church, its outline has been preserved where it once stood, built into the end wall of what is now The Prince of Wales pub.

Address The Prince of Wales, 81–83 St Mary Street, Cardiff, CF10 1FA | **Getting there** Bus to Cardiff Bus Interchange; train to Cardiff Central | **Hours** Viewable from the outside only; pub open Fri & Sat 8am–1am, Sun–Thu 8am–midnight | **Tip** St John's Church was built as a chapel of ease for St Mary's and took over as the main church when St Mary's was closed. It remains open to visitors (www.stjohnscardiff.wales).

101 St Teilo's Skull

The world's most travelled relic?

The first indication of Llandaff Cathedral's claim to supremacy is found in the number of saints it is dedicated to – no fewer than five! These are St Peter, St Paul, St Dyfrig, St Teilo and St Euddogwy. And not one, but two of these have their relics in the cathedral.

As the first primate of the diocese, St Dyfrig has his own chapel. He was initially buried on Bardsey Island where he died, but his relics were moved to Llandaff on the founding of the cathedral by the Normans in 1120.

The other relics have travelled somewhat further. Well, part of them, at least. St Teilo was the second bishop of the diocese, from the 6th century. Although his body has always resided in the cathedral, the bishop gave the skull to the Mathew family in 1450, to thank them for looking after the saint's shrine. St Teilo remained headless for centuries, during which time the church lost track of the skull's whereabouts. In the 1990s, over half a millennium after it was last in the cathedral, it was found in Australia, mounted in silver as a drinking cup.

In 1994, it was returned to Llandaff Cathedral, posing a conundrum for the now Anglican church, as, unlike Catholics, Anglicans do not venerate relics. After some discussion, the authorities decided to compromise. It is stored in its own niche, protected by a sealed glass screen to avoid tarnishing. However, the niche is tucked away and behind closed wooden doors. This enables Catholics to visit the relics, without them being obvious to the everyday congregation.

More obvious is the *Majestas pulpita*, added when the cathedral was repaired after World War II bomb damage. The church wanted something to add mystery (and presumably majesty), breaking up the view to the end of the building, while allowing the congregation to see the Norman arch beyond. Whether you love it or hate it, it certainly fulfils the brief.

Address Llandaff Cathedral, Cathedral Close, Cardiff, CF5 2LA, +44 (0) 292 056 4554, www.llandaffcathedral.org.uk, admin@llandaffcathedral.org.uk | Getting there Train to Waun-Gron Park (17-minute walk); bus 1, 2 or M1 to Cardiff Met Llandaff | Hours Daily (see website for times) | Tip 100 metres uphill from the east end of the cathedral, St Teilo's Well is on Cathedral Close. The Celtic cross in the cathedral, which predates the church itself, was found in 1870, built into the wall behind the well.

102_Temple of Peace

'A peace building for peacebuilding'

Serving in the trenches during World War I, Lord Davies of Llandinam was so horrified that he wanted to set up a memorial for all those lost in the war, and promote peace and good health for future generations. His first proposal was for a Temple of Peace and Health in London, but the idea was rejected. Not one to give up easily, he turned to his homeland instead. In 1928, when the Welsh National War Memorial was unveiled, he proposed a Welsh Temple of Peace and Health in the nearby civic quarter.

On approval, he commissioned Welsh architect Percy Thomas to design a building that would be a suitable home for Wales' World War I Book of Remembrance and as a 'memorial to the future'. His family's money largely funded the construction with a donation of £60,000, topped up with public subscriptions amounting to £12,000.

Ten years later, this spectacular 1930s Art Deco building was opened by Minnie James, who was there to represent the mothers of those lost to war worldwide. Sadly, it was only a matter of months before the world was back at war.

The building was not hit during the blitzes of World War II but, ironically, for a building in which people worked for peace, it did suffer bomb damage later in its life. The first of five incendiary devices associated with the investiture of HRH Prince Charles as Prince of Wales was detonated at the building, causing damage to the vestibule.

The building's guardian is now the Welsh Centre for International Affairs, a charity set up in the 1970s with a vision of 'a Wales where every person contributes to creating a fairer and more peaceful world'. Their use of the building as a venue for private events and by film crews (you might recognise the building from *Doctor Who* or *His Dark Materials*) helps to pay for its upkeep and the charity's work in maintaining and developing Wales' global influence on peaceful living.

Address King Edward VII Avenue, Cardiff, CF10 3AP, +44 (0) 292 022 8549, www.templeofpeace.wales, bookings@wcia.org.uk | Getting there Several buses to College Road or Corbett Road; train to Cardiff Central (25-minute walk); on-site parking | Hours Open for scheduled tours only; reservation required | Tip There are several other spectacular buildings in the civic quarter. Walk towards the city centre to admire the Crown Court and City Hall (www.cardiffcityhall.com).

103 Terrapin Island

Pets and pests

The Teenage Mutant Ninja Turtles have a lot to answer for. Conceived in the 1980s as comic book characters, it was not long before they became screen hits. As a result, children pestered parents for terrapins, and parents caved in. Terrapins quickly grow from a cute little animal that easily fits into the palm of a child's hand into something closer to the size of a dinner plate. They cannot be petted and take a lot of looking after; they need large ponds or tanks, lamps for heating and lighting, and a mixed diet that includes different types of fish, amphibians, rodents, birds, eggs and plants. And, if this all already sounds tricky, they also live for a long time, typically 30 to 40 years. Combining all of these factors, the craze for terrapins as pets was bound to run into trouble.

Once the challenges of terrapin ownership became evident, many impulse purchasers dumped them in lakes around the UK. Although their natural environment is far warmer than ours, so many survived that they have become classified as an 'invasive alien species' because of the impact they can have on local wildlife.

At the first sign of trouble, terrapins slide into the water. Once there, they are challenging to catch. However, some terrapins released into Roath Park Lake were successfully caught and rehomed in Roath Park Conservatory. Here, they have plenty of space and a warm environment, similar to their native habitat. Because they bask during the day to warm themselves up, they can usually be seen on the rocky island in the large conservatory pond. The pond is also home to a pair of whistling ducks and several varieties of colourful koi carp and goldfish.

Other attractions in the conservatory include exotic plants, such as an arabica coffee bush, a black pepper plant, banana plants and orchids. However, the terrapins remain a firm favourite with visitors.

Address Roath Park Botanic Gardens, Cardiff, CF23 5PG | Getting there Bus 28 or 29 to Lady Mary Road | Hours See website for seasonal hours | Tip To the west of the conservatory, Cathays Cemetery has some interesting graves, including that belonging to a pioneer of airship flight and a Cardiff boxer who forewent a title fight in aid of charity. A fascinating heritage trail has been devised for visitors (https://cathayscemetery.coffeecup.com).

104 Tiny Forest

A space for all seasons

There is little doubt that drastic action is needed to respond to the nature and climate crisis that is unfolding worldwide, and many options are being considered. One of the available options is to create tiny forests like this one on the Cardiff Bay Barrage.

Tiny forests are planted with copious numbers of trees in a small area. The mix is chosen to reflect the species and structure of a native forest. Because they are planted so densely, they rapidly grow into thriving forest ecosystems despite the diminutive size of the plot.

This small 100-square-metre area of Cardiff Barrage was planted with around 1,000 trees of 25 different species. This guarantees interest for visitors all year round. In spring, the green of the new hawthorn leaves would give a high-vis jacket a run for its money. The hawthorn and other trees also provide a show of blossom, which fills the air like confetti on a breezy day. In summer, the forest offers an oasis of cool, and the trees release feel-good volatile organic compounds into the air. At this time of year, the trees are, of course, in full leaf, and the aspen leaves, in particular, tremble in the slightest of breezes. In autumn, colour and interest are offered by fruit, including bunches of deep-red haws and colourful crab apples, and leaves turning to shades of yellow and gold before carpeting the ground. And the show does not stop when winter arrives. The brightly coloured stems of dogwood and the white trunks of silver birch contrast with the darker shades of a winter woodland. Look out, too, for the small, waxy magenta and orange flowers that adorn the spindle bushes.

It is not only human visitors that thrive with such a rich variety of trees. Birds flit around in the canopy and butterflies and bees on the flowers. A closer inspection may also unearth mini-beasts such as woodlice, beetles, spiders and the many-legged centipedes and millipedes.

Address Cargo Road, Cardiff, CF10 4LY | **Getting there** Train to Cardiff Bay; bus 305 to Barrage (17-minute walk from Penarth end of barrage) or bus 1, 1A, 8 or X2 to Mermaid Quay (20-minute walk) | **Hours** Accessible 24 hours | **Tip** A tower next to the forest plays the sound of swifts in the hope of attracting others here to nest.

105 Tiny Rebel

The boozy bear with a big heart

The pub signs attached to this Victorian building give a strong clue about the nature of the bar inside. It is a thoroughly modern rebellion, bringing craft beer with attitude to the heart of the capital. The bar's story began in Newport, where friends Brad and Gazz started brewing in a garage in 2012. Their experimental approach led to recipes that quickly gained attention, and Tiny Rebel has since become Wales' largest independent craft brewery. The accolades followed, including 'Champion Beer of Britain' and 'SIBA Brewery Business of the Year'.

The Cardiff venue made its mark immediately, winning *ShortList* magazine's 'Best New Bar' in its first year. Its central location makes it a popular spot, although you might struggle to get in on match days, when it quickly fills with rugby fans. Despite its success, it maintains the approachable, quirky atmosphere of an independent, with street art-style decor and a relaxed vibe.

The bar showcases Tiny Rebel's innovative range, which has frequent new additions, including alcohol-free options. Alongside their own creations, they serve carefully chosen guest ales. The menu is based on burgers, so this is not the place to go if you are after fancy food, although it does offer a range of vegan alternatives.

Despite its rebellious nature, or maybe because of it, this is a brewery that takes its responsibilities seriously. Its community fund supports local projects, while staff benefits include everything from a cycle-to-work scheme to profit sharing. It's an approach that shows how craft-beer culture can be a force for positive change. What started as a Tiny Rebellion has become a Cardiff institution, but hasn't lost its edge. Brad and Gazz's mission to 'bring you great times and great beer' has evolved into something bigger, proving that success and social conscience can go hand in hand with a really good pint.

Address 25 Westgate Street, Cardiff, CF10 1DD, +44 (0) 7377 414204, www.tinyrebel.co.uk/bars/cardiff, cardiffbar@tinyrebelbars.co.uk | Getting there Several buses to Westgate Street; train to Cardiff Central | Hours Sun–Wed noon–1am, Thu–Sat noon–2am; food Mon–Sat noon–9pm, Sun noon–6pm | Tip If Tiny Rebel beers don't tickle your fancy, there are plenty of alternative establishments on neighbouring Womanby Street.

106_Treetop Adventure Golf

Putting through paradise

As you enter Treetop Adventure Golf, you are presented with a delightful dilemma: will you navigate the lush dangers of the Tropical Trail, putting past poisonous frogs and navigating the Mighty Oracle Tree, or will you face the enigmatic challenges of Ancient Explorer's cryptic ruins and sacred spirits?

Bright, bold and brassy, there is nothing natural about these courses, except for the golfers' competitive instincts. Both courses offer immersive themed environments where exaggeration and entertainment are the order of the day. Atmospheric lighting and sound effects complete the illusion of walking through a cartoon film set. Even the golf is like Goldilocks – not too easy, not too hard, but just right.

On the Tropical Trail, you will encounter exotic wildlife, some obvious like the poisonous frogs guarding the green, and some hidden away in the dense rainforest foliage – keep your eyes open for surprises! Vines wind their way up the trunk of the Mighty Oracle Tree and dangle from its outstretched branches, lit in colourful shades of magenta, emerald and azure. Nearby, the Ancient Tree Spirit smiles benignly from another trunk, his eyes boring into those approaching along the green. On the Ancient Explorer course, it is stone serpents and sacred spirits that guard the route. Cryptic carvings and crumbling ruins add to the sense of being immersed in an archaeological dig, playing your part in uncovering an ancient civilisation.

If time is on your side, there is no dilemma – you can challenge yourself to complete both routes. And the 19th hole offers the chance to win another game, too. After the game is over, the experience continues. In this jungle, the residents eat wonky pizzas at Pizza Cabana, tuck into shakes, locally roasted coffee and sweet treats at the Jungle Buzz Café, and sup local beers, colourful cocktails and mocktails in the Thirsty Toucan bar.

Address St David's Centre, Cardiff, CF10 2EQ, www.adventuregolf.com/cardiff | Getting there Train to Cardiff Queen Street or Cardiff Central; several buses to Canal Street. Access by the Treetop lifts on ground floor or level 1, or follow signs from level P3 of the car park | Hours See website for hours | Tip For an edgier adventure-golf experience, head over to Golf Fang in the Brewery Quarter (www.golffang.co.uk/cardiff).

107 Victoria Park Splash Pad

A cool place to play

Most parents would agree that having children is an expensive business and that finding activities to entertain them during the school holidays can be stressful. In Cardiff, one popular solution to that conundrum is the splash pad at Victoria Park.

Here, children can spend as much time as they like running around, dodging water sprays and jets – or squealing with delight as they run through them on a hot summer's day. The colossal bucket on stilts is a favourite. As it fills with water, the space underneath fills with children. The tension mounts as faces are turned upwards, eyes watching as the bucket starts to lean, trying to determine the exact moment when gravity will take control. Just a few more seconds… and boom! It's tipped, water is spraying everywhere, and shrieks can be heard across the park as the frigid water hits.

Eventually, even the most enthusiastic and hardy child is ready for a break, at which point they can climb around the play area to warm up and then cool down again with an ice cream from the kiosk.

The splash pad sits near the statue of Billy the Seal in the centre of the park, positioned to make the most of the sun. However, the park also has plenty of shade provided by the now-mature trees planted by the Victorians. Families often spread blankets on the grass beneath these leafy giants for a summer picnic, sheltered from the hot summer sun.

For older children and adults, Victoria Park also has tennis courts and a multi-use games area. In 2022, these were joined by purpose-built beach volleyball courts using imported sand. Since beach volleyball became an Olympic sport, its popularity has soared. Even though this is a city location with the nearest sandy beach some distance away, the courts have proved to be popular. The beach volleyball club is thriving, and the facility is even used for major sporting events.

Address Cowbridge Road East, Cardiff, CF5 1EH, www.outdoorcardiff.com/parks/victoria-park | Getting there Several buses to Victoria Park; train to Waun-Gron Park (16-minute walk) or Ninian Park (20-minute walk) | Hours See website for seasonal hours | Tip Pettigrew Bakery is opposite the entrance to the park and popular for its sausage rolls and hot chocolate (www.pettigrew-bakeries.co.uk).

108_Vulcan Hotel

The last of Little Ireland

Although the government does not consider this building important enough to be protected by listing, there was a public outcry when it was going to be demolished to redevelop the area where it stood – Cardiffians did want to protect it. This reaction ultimately led to its deconstruction in 2012 and reconstruction, brick by brick, tile by tile, and urinal by urinal in St Fagans National Museum of History. It reopened as a working pub in 2024.

The first Irish workers arrived in Cardiff by invitation of the Marquess of Bute. His Welsh workers were on strike, and he wanted to complete the construction of West Dock. That they arrived to break a strike immediately made them unpopular. A few years later, the Potato Famine of 1845 led to a further influx of workers from Ireland. These received free passage as ships' ballast, as they were faster to load and unload than the traditional stones used for that purpose. Hungry and desperate, they would do any work they were offered, at lower rates than the local workers. Although understandable, this generated more resentment among Cardiffians as all wages and housing standards dropped. In this atmosphere, many of the Irish immigrants took housing together, creating a community that became known as 'Little Ireland'.

The Vulcan Hotel, named after the Roman god of fire because of a nearby ironworks, is the only building from Little Ireland that remains standing. Opened in 1853, it served the local population at shift changes, whatever time of day or night. The hotel was significantly remodelled around 1901 and updated again in 1914. The brown and green tiles that characterise the pub now were added at that time, along with the urinals. Originally, the latter were outside in the courtyard, washed by rain and aired by the wind. Unfortunately, they are no longer quite as well ventilated, and they can sometimes smell their age!

Address St Fagans National Museum of History, Cardiff, CF5 6XB, www.museum.wales/stfagans, stfagans@museumwales.ac.uk | **Getting there** Bus 320 or 32 to St Fagans Church; on-site parking | **Hours** See website for seasonal hours | **Tip** The Plymouth Arms pub in St Fagans village is a popular alternative to the on-site café (www.vintageinn.co.uk).

109 Weird and Wonderful Wales Mural

A steamy story

The water tower at Cardiff Central Station was built in the 1930s to supply water from the river to steam engines on the Fish Platform. It was not long before Great Western Railway started to replace steam locomotives with diesel engines, and the tower became obsolete.

It has had several decorations over the decades, but only the latest has featured Welsh legends. It was created as a part of the 'Weird and Wonderful Wales' project, which explored legends associated with Cadw sites and culminated in the production of this mural, inspired by the characters of the Mabinogion.

The Mabinogion is a collection of ancient Welsh tales, passed down the generations aurally until they were first written down in medieval times. The Weird and Wonderful Wales Mural features several characters, including Bendigeidfran, the King of Britain whose severed head continued to talk to his men; Rhiannon, a goddess who is a skilled horsewoman; and Blodeuwedd, the owl, who is the subject of a steamy story.

The character Lleu's mother has doomed him never to have a human wife, so a couple of magicians conjure a non-human wife for him from the flowers of broom, meadowsweet and oak. This origin story gave her the name Blodeuwedd, which means 'flower-faced'. Blodeuwedd, perhaps not bound by human scruples but very human in temperament, has an affair and plans to kill Lleu to free her from their marriage. She fails, and the magicians who created her in the first place punish her by turning her into an owl, as owls do not see the light of day and are hated by all other birds.

Whatever you might consider the moral of the story to be, Blodeuwedd now flies on the water tower in pride of place, as a reminder to all who look at it of Welsh culture and the importance of those stories of old.

Address Stadium Plaza, Wood Street, Cardiff, CF10 1LA | Getting there Train to Cardiff Central; several buses to Cardiff Bridge | Hours Viewable from the outside only | Tip From here, it is possible to do a short circular walk along the river past the stadium, crossing at Cardiff Bridge and returning on the far side. Alternatively, cross and turn left to walk downstream all the way to Cardiff Bay.

110 Whitchurch Common Trees

An arboreal memorial

During World War II, Whitchurch Common looked somewhat different to how it does today. A bomb had left an enormous crater, and the ground was rocky and uneven. The common housed an air-raid shelter, several huts, and a large static tank for water to be used to douse fires.

For almost four months around the time of the Normandy landings, members of the 2nd Evacuation Unit of the US Army were based in Whitchurch. As with other members of the US Army who stayed in Cardiff, most were billeted with families and were popular guests. By this stage, the UK had been at war for several years, and the luxuries and cheer the American soldiers brought with them and shared with local people were welcomed. The 2nd Evacuation Unit specialised in setting up tented field hospitals that could be rapidly deployed and relocated. The unit did not stay for long, as they followed Germany's retreat through France after the Allies' invasion, providing tented hospital services to injured soldiers. Their expertise proved invaluable during the challenging months following D-Day.

At the end of the war, the unit's response to the hospitality they received in Whitchurch was also welcomed – a donation that paid for over 250 trees to be planted on the common. The trees were chosen, and an avenue that was three rows deep was planted. They were officially presented by the American consul in Cardiff in 1948. Over subsequent years, work on the trees has resulted in a less formal structure now being in place, but nevertheless, a dense canopy of trees lines the road.

After the war, the land was transferred into council ownership, levelled and planted with grass. The mature trees provide welcome shade in the summer and a habitat for wildlife, serving as a living memorial to the connection between Whitchurch residents and their American guests.

Address Merthyr Road, Whitchurch, Cardiff, CF14 1JE | Getting there Several buses to Ararat Church; train to Llandaf (21-minute walk) or Rhiwbina (24-minute walk) | Hours Accessible 24 hours | Tip To grab some pub grub, head to the popular Three Elms at the far (western) end of the Common.

111 World's Smallest Lovespoon

It's not the size that counts!

Imagine being a man in the 17th century and wanting to communicate your love for your sweetheart in a lasting way. What can you do? You can't write a letter – neither of you can read or write. You can't create a playlist for them or take them to the Seychelles for a romantic marriage proposal.

One thing you can do, though, is make things. You eat using wooden spoons, so you are skilled at carving them. Perhaps you could carve one and make it a little more intricate than an everyday spoon. Perhaps you could even sell yourself as a suitable husband through this process.

And that is precisely what Welsh men started to do. They carved hearts into spoon handles to show their love. They carved links to highlight their desire for connection. We think that balls in cages indicated the number of children they wanted, that wheels suggested a willingness to work hard, and that diamonds promised either luck or wealth. The amount of effort expended in making the spoon indicated their dedication.

Modern lovespoons come in a wide variety of styles and are made by men, women and machines. You can even get them made in chocolate, although that medium seems a little short-lived for an expression of eternal love!

Castle Welsh Crafts opposite the castle displays a selection of historical lovespoons, as well as handcrafted spoons to buy. The largest known lovespoon at the time of carving dominates the shop, crossing the ceiling and dropping down the wall. The smallest in the world is less easy to spot in a small presentation case, with a matchstick for scale. Other spoons are made from ancient wood or engraved in delicate patterns.

Whether you're a romantic at heart or simply looking for a perfect gift, Welsh lovespoons offer something special – an abiding expression of love that is as relevant today as it was in the 17th century.

Address Castle Welsh Crafts, 1–3 Castle Street, Cardiff, CF10 1BS, www.castlewelshcrafts.co.uk, thewelshshop@castlewelshcrafts.co.uk | Getting there Bus 44, 45, 49 or 50 to Castle Street; train to Cardiff Central | Hours Mon–Sat 9.30am–5.30pm, Sun 10am–4.30pm | Tip The oldest known Welsh lovespoon can be seen at St Fagans National Museum of History (www.museum.wales/stfagans).

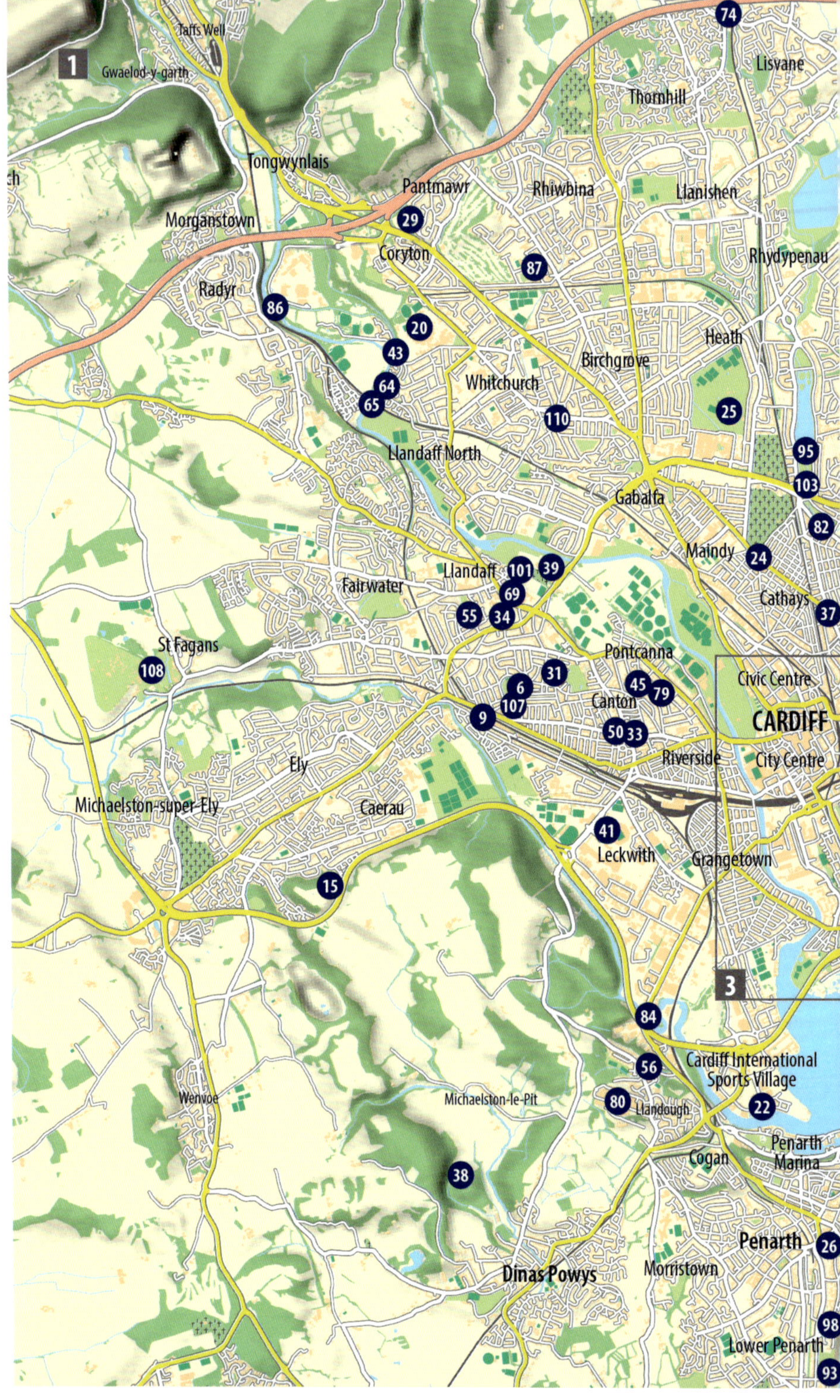

1
Taffs Well
Gwaelod-y-garth
74
Lisvane
Thornhill
Tongwynlais
Pantmawr
Rhiwbina
Llanishen
Morganstown
29
Coryton
Rhydypenau
87
Radyr
86
20
Heath
43
Birchgrove
64
Whitchurch
65
110
25
Llandaff North
95
103
Gabalfa
82
Maindy
24
Llandaff
101
39
Fairwater
69
Cathays
55
34
37
St Fagans
Pontcanna
108
31
Civic Centre
6
45
79
107
Canton
CARDIFF
9
50
33
Riverside
City Centre
Ely
Michaelston-super-Ely
Caerau
41
Leckwith
Grangetown
15
3
84
Cardiff International Sports Village
56
Wenvoe
Michaelston-le-Pit
80
Llandough
22
Cogan
Penarth Marina
38
Penarth
26
Dinas Powys
Morristown
98
Lower Penarth
93

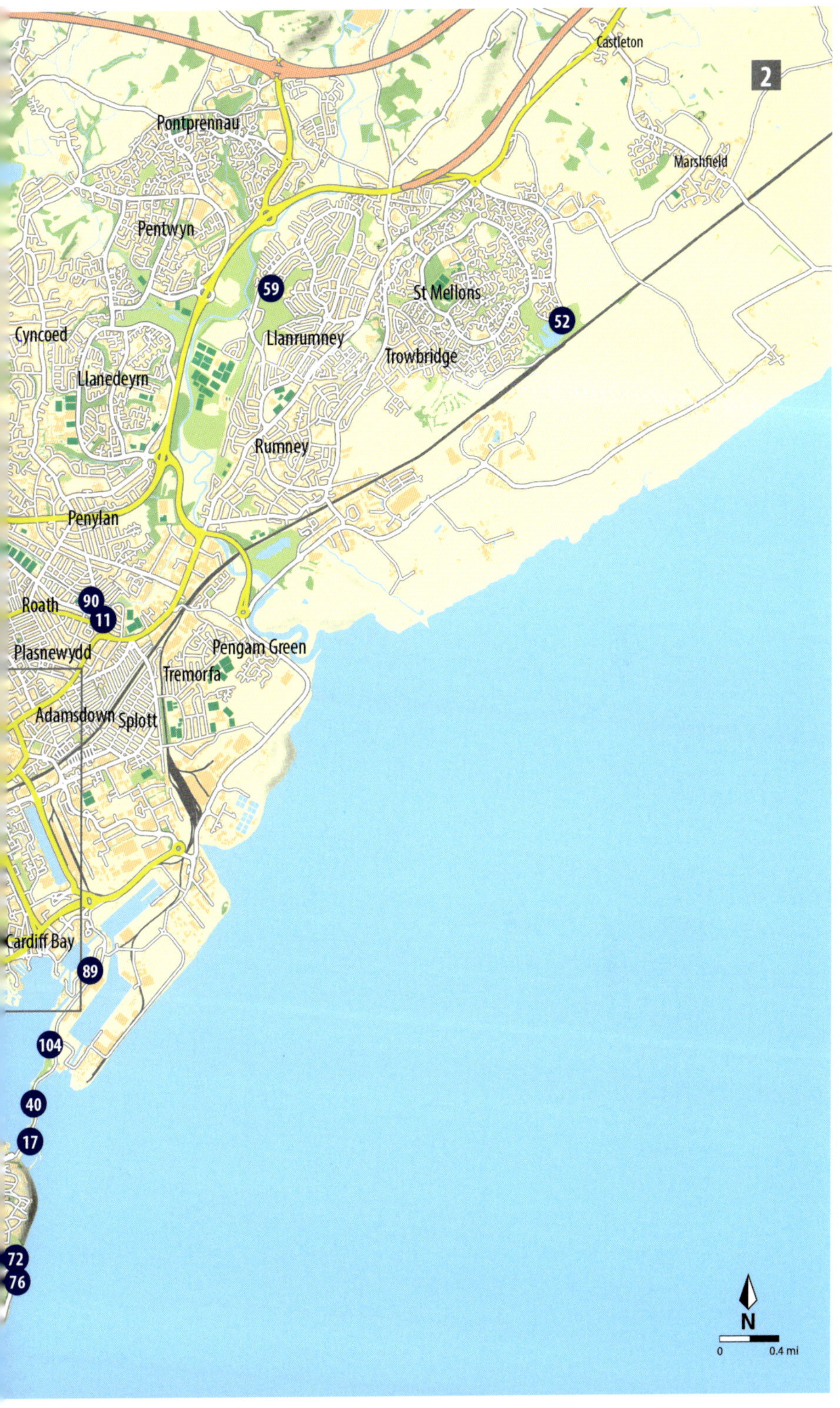
2
Castleton
Pontprennau
Marshfield
Pentwyn
59
St Mellons
52
Cyncoed
Llanrumney
Trowbridge
Llanedeyrn
Rumney
Penylan
Roath
90
11
Plasnewydd
Pengam Green
Tremorfa
Adamsdown
Splott
Cardiff Bay
89
104
40
17
72
76
N
0
0.4 mi

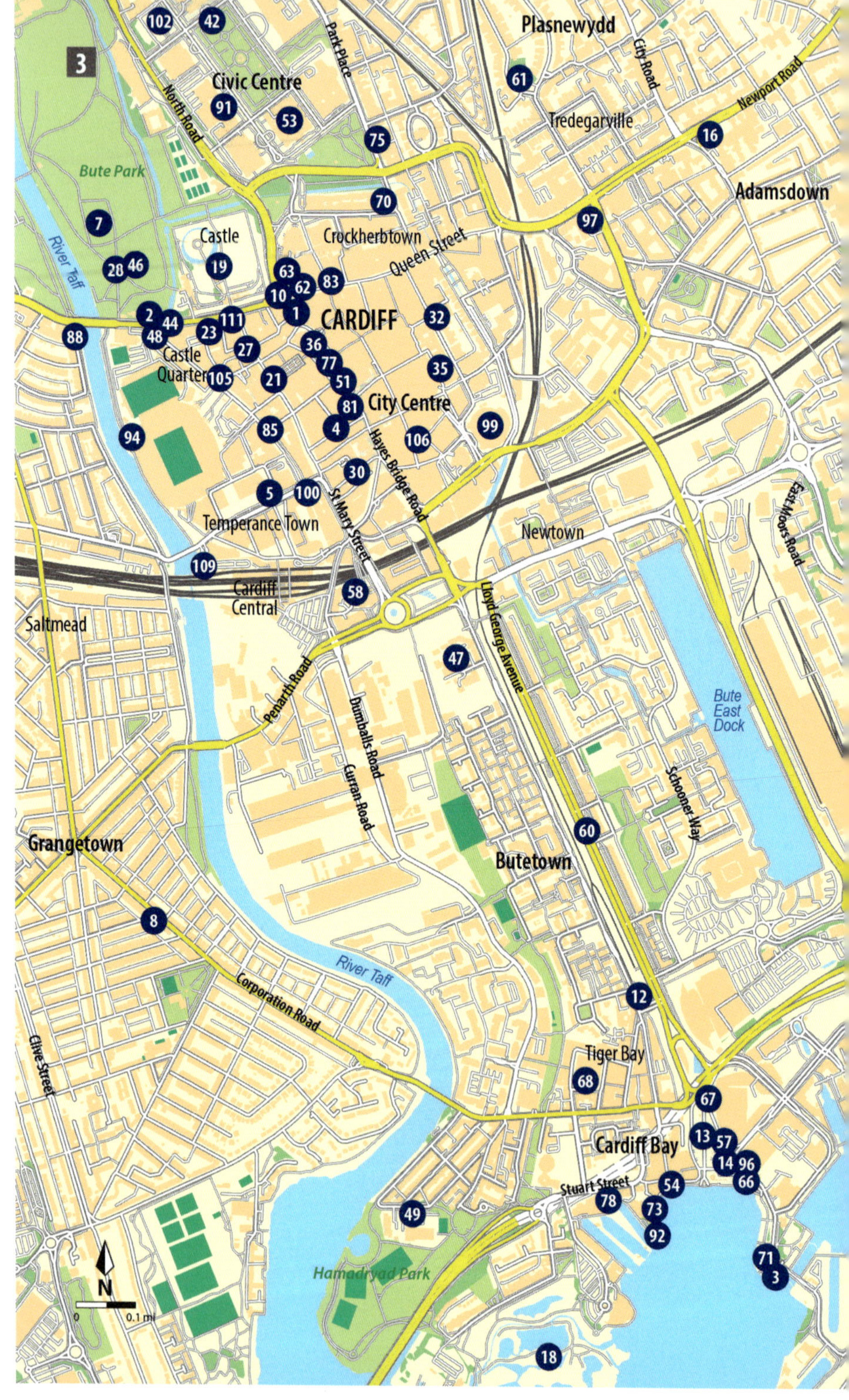
3
Civic Centre
Plasnewydd
Park Place
North Road
City Road
Tredegarville
Newport Road
Bute Park
Adamsdown
Castle
Crockherbtown
Queen Street
River Taff
CARDIFF
Castle Quarter
City Centre
Hayes Bridge Road
St Mary Street
Temperance Town
Newtown
East Moors Road
Cardiff Central
Saltmead
Penarth Road
Lloyd George Avenue
Dumballs Road
Curran Road
Bute East Dock
Schooner Way
Grangetown
Butetown
River Taff
Corporation Road
Tiger Bay
Clive Street
Cardiff Bay
Stuart Street
Hamadryad Park
N
0
0.1 mi

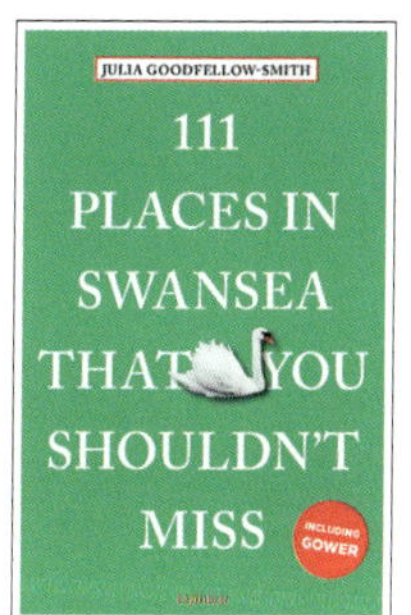

Julia Goodfellow Smith
111 Places in Swansea That You Shouldn't Miss
ISBN 978-3-7408-2065-7

Catriona Neil, Adrian Spalding
111 Places in Cornwall That You Shouldn't Miss
ISBN 978-3-7408-2805-9

Martin Booth, Barbara Evripidou
111 Places in Bristol That You Shouldn't Miss
ISBN 978-3-7408-2512-6

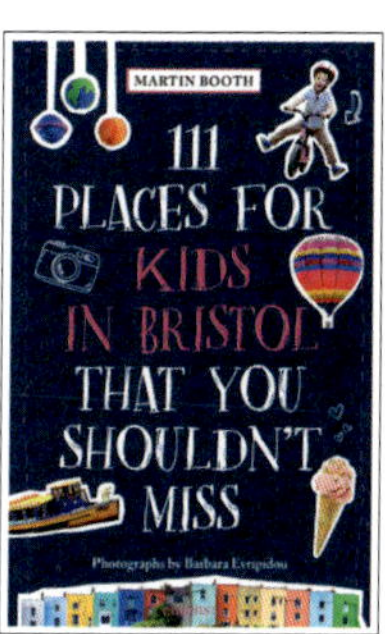

Martin Booth, Barbara Evripidou
111 Places for Kids in Bristol That You Shouldn't Miss
ISBN 978-3-7408-1665-0

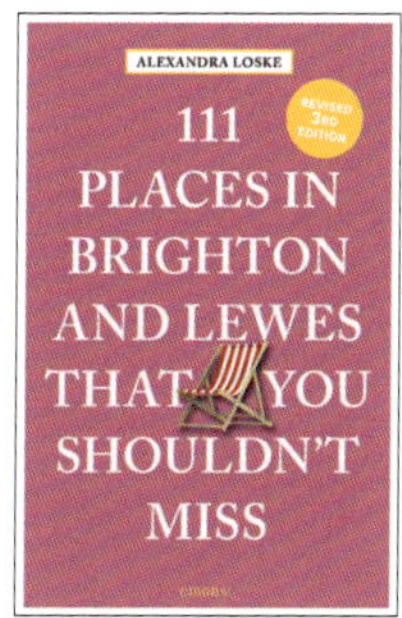

Alexandra Loske
111 Places in Brighton and Lewes That You Shouldn't Miss
ISBN 978-3-7408-1727-5

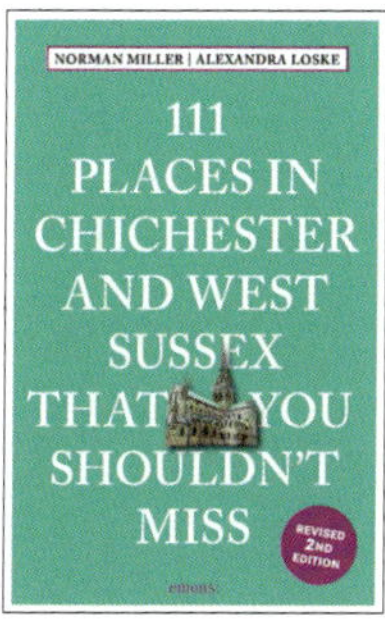

Norman Miller, Alexandra Loske
111 Places in Chichester and West Sussex That You Shouldn't Miss
ISBN 978-3-7408-2807-3

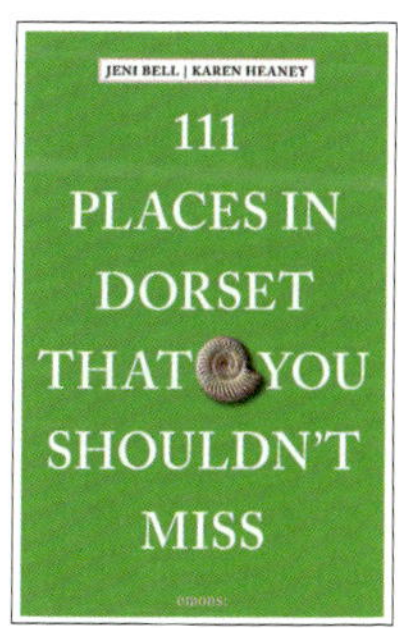

Jeni Bell, Karen Heaney
111 Places in Dorset That You Shouldn't Miss
ISBN 978-3-7408-2146-3

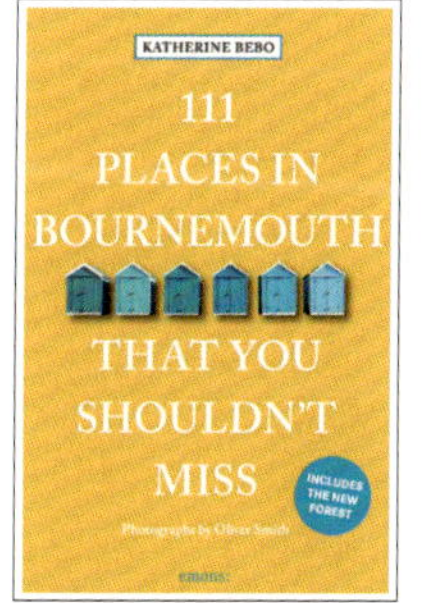

Katherine Bebo, Oliver Smith
111 Places in Bournemouth That You Shouldn't Miss
ISBN 978-3-7408-2646-8

Katherine Bebo, Oliver Smith
111 Places in Poole That You Shouldn't Miss
ISBN 978-3-7408-0598-2

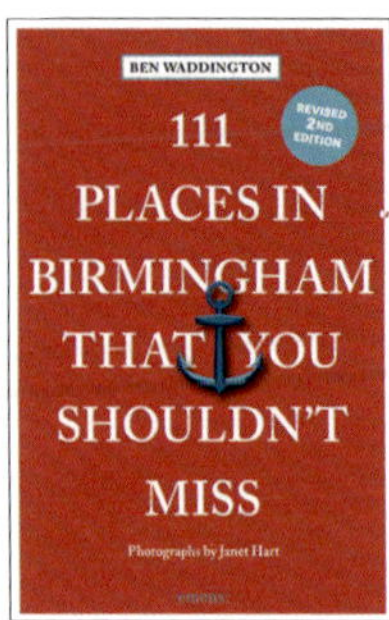

Ben Waddington, Janet Hart
111 Places in Birmingham That You Shouldn't Miss
ISBN 978-3-7408-2268-2

Solange Berchemin
111 Places in the Lake District That You Shouldn't Miss
ISBN 978-3-7408-2824-0

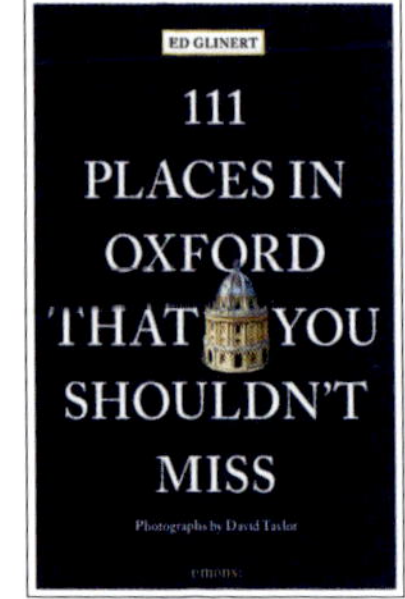

Ed Glinert, David Taylor
111 Places in Oxford That You Shouldn't Miss
ISBN 978-3-7408-1990-3

David Taylor
111 Places in Newcastle That You Shouldn't Miss
ISBN 978-3-7408-1043-6

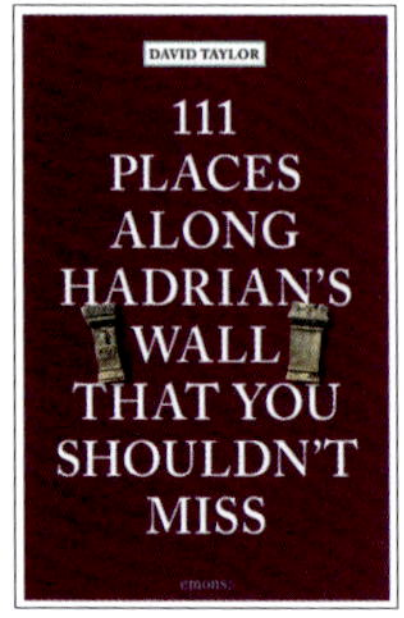

David Taylor
111 Places along Hadrian's Wall That You Shouldn't Miss
ISBN 978-3-7408-1425-0

David Taylor
111 Places in Northumberland That You Shouldn't Miss
ISBN 978-3-7408-1792-3

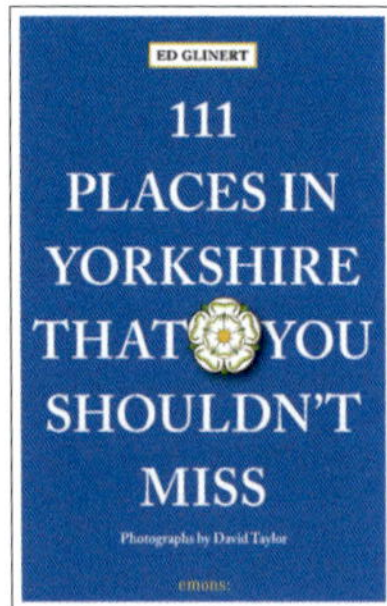

Ed Glinert, David Taylor
111 Places in Yorkshire That You Shouldn't Miss
ISBN 978-3-7408-1167-9

Ed Glinert, Karin Tearle
111 Places in Essex That You Shouldn't Miss
ISBN 978-3-7408-1593-6

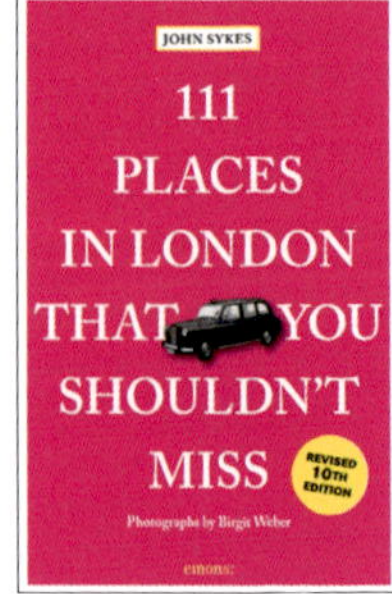

John Sykes, Birgit Weber
111 Places in London That You Shouldn't Miss
ISBN 978-3-7408-2379-5

Alicia Edwards
111 Places for Kids in London That You Shouldn't Miss
ISBN 978-3-7408-2196-8

Michael Glover, Benedict Flett
111 Hidden Art Treasures in London That You Shouldn't Miss
ISBN 978-3-7408-1576-9

Terry Philpot, Karin Tearle
111 Literary Places in London That You Shouldn't Miss
ISBN 978-3-7408-1954-5

Ed Glinert, Marc Zakian
111 Places in London's East End That You Shouldn't Miss
ISBN 978-3-7408-0752-8

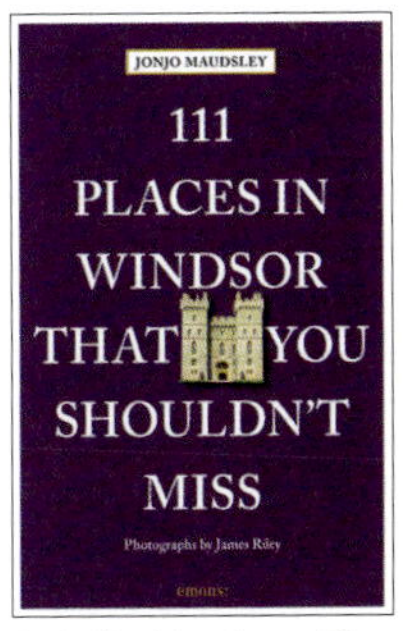

Jonjo Maudsley, James Riley
111 Places in Windsor That You Shouldn't Miss
ISBN 978-3-7408-2009-1

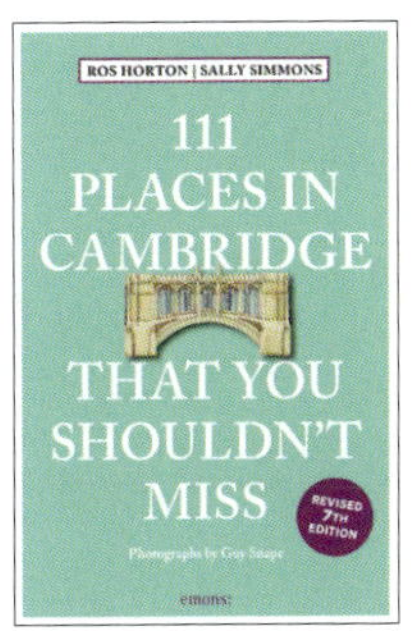

Rosalind Horton, Sally Simmons, Guy Snape
111 Places in Cambridge That You Shouldn't Miss
ISBN 978-3-7408-2376-4

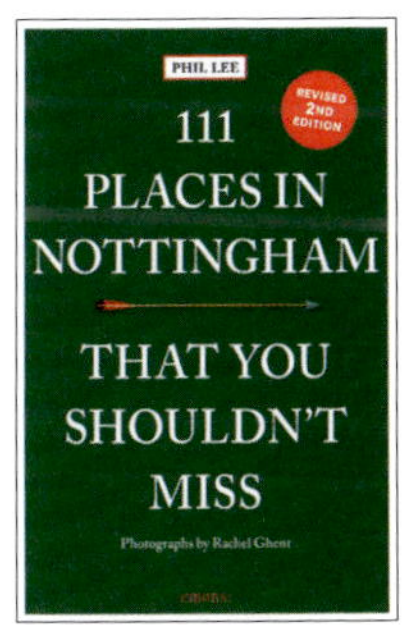

Phil Lee, Rachel Ghent
111 Places in Nottingham That You Shouldn't Miss
ISBN 978-3-7408-2261-3

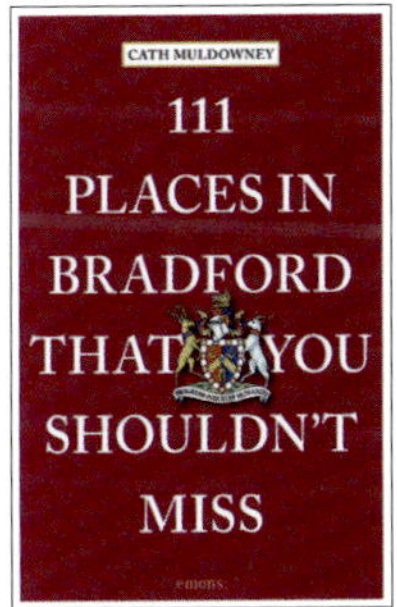

Cath Muldowney
111 Places in Bradford That You Shouldn't Miss
ISBN 978-3-7408-1427-4

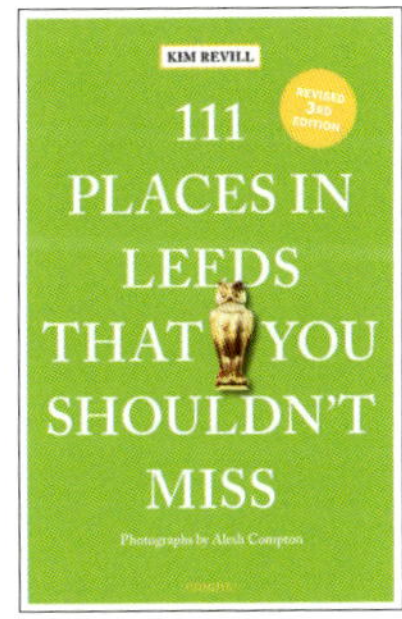

Kim Revill, Alesh Compton
111 Places in Leeds That You Shouldn't Miss
ISBN 978-3-7408-2059-6

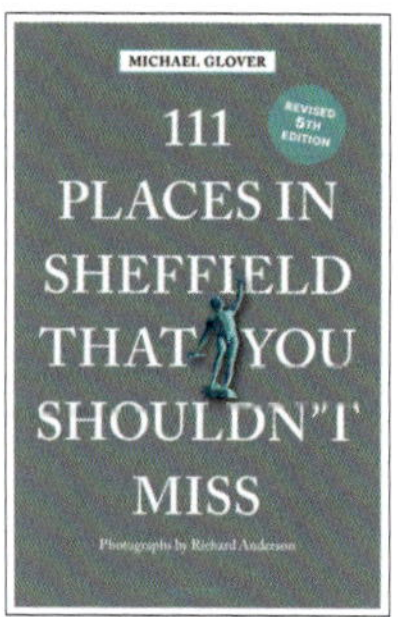

Michael Glover, Richard Anderson
111 Places in Sheffield That You Shouldn't Miss
ISBN 978-3-7408-2348-1

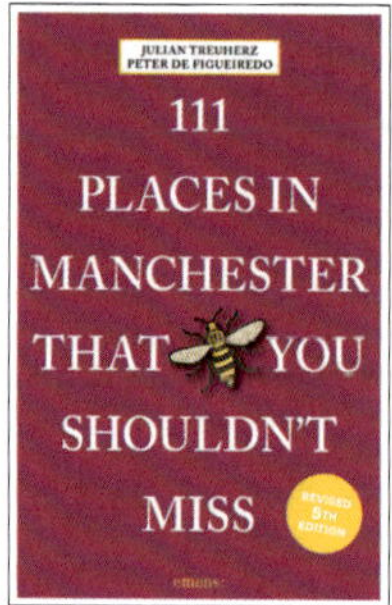

Julian Treuherz, Peter de Figueiredo
111 Places in Manchester That You Shouldn't Miss
ISBN 978-3-7408-2645-1

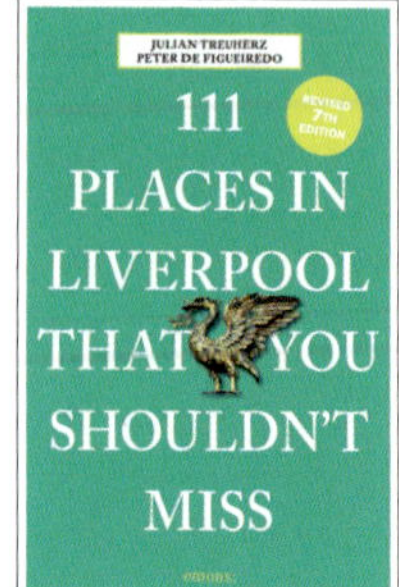

Julian Treuherz, Peter de Figueiredo
111 Places in Liverpool That You Shouldn't Miss
ISBN 978-3-7408-2515-7

Philip R. Stone
111 Dark Places in England That You Shouldn't Miss
ISBN 978-3-7408-0900-3

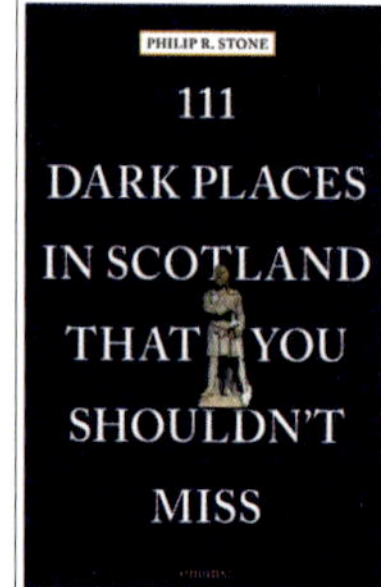

Philip R. Stone
111 Dark Places in Scotland That You Shouldn't Miss
ISBN 978-3-7408-1895-1

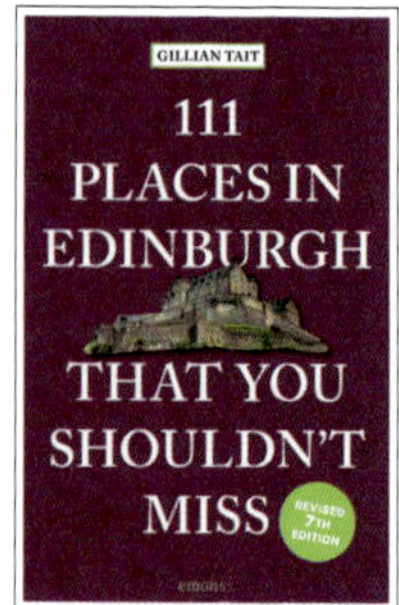

Gillian Tait
111 Places in Edinburgh That You Shouldn't Miss
ISBN 978-3-7408-2575-1

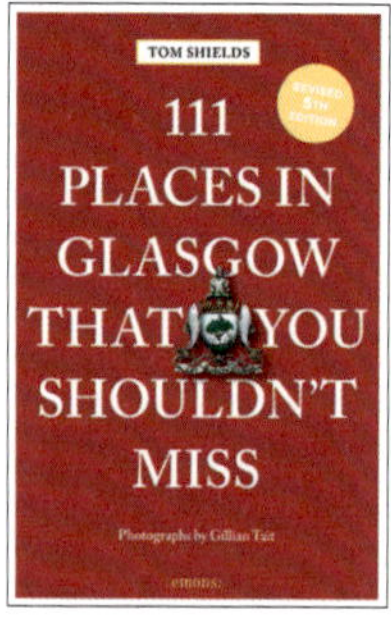

Tom Shields, Gillian Tait
111 Places in Glasgow That You Shouldn't Miss
ISBN 978-3-7408-2237-8

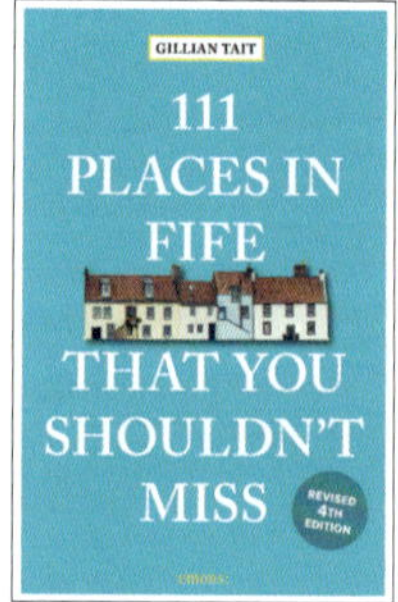

Gillian Tait
111 Places in Fife That You Shouldn't Miss
ISBN 978-3-7408-2806-6

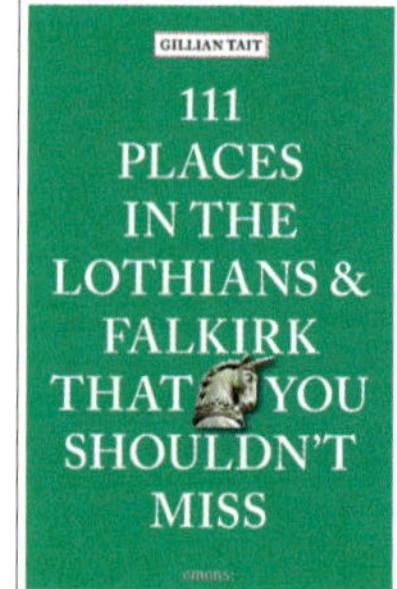

Gillian Tait
111 Places in the Lothians and Falkirk That You Shouldn't Miss
ISBN 978-3-7408-1569-1

Acknowledgements

Although mine is the only name that appears on the cover of this book, it has been a team effort to bring it to fruition. First, I must thank my friends who know Cardiff well and suggested places to consider for inclusion: Kevin, Julie, Ieuan, Alison and Matthew, my hairdresser. Ieuan and Alison very kindly gave me somewhere to stay while I was researching the book, too – thank you.

Then there are the tour guides, journalists, authors, librarians and venue managers who helped me with my research and photography. Thank you.

Much of the book's production happens behind the scenes at the publisher – Laura Olk, who commissioned me to write this and other *111 Places* books, Tania Taylor, who patiently queried and edited the manuscript, Katherine Bebo, the diligent proof-reader, the photo editors, page formatters, marketers and anyone else I have unwittingly missed from the list – thank you.

My husband, Mike, has not only provided encouragement and hot meals but also contributed to the research and photography. Without you, none of this would be possible. Thank you.

Julia Goodfellow-Smith is an author and photographer. When she moved to Llanelli, she started exploring South Wales, mainly on foot. She discovered a love for the area and a desire to know more. In this book, she shares some of the unexpected treasures she found in her ventures in Cardiff. Julia is the author of several books, including *111 Places in Swansea That You Shouldn't Miss, The Walker's Guide to the Castles of Britain, Top 10 Walks: Coastal Pub Walks – South Wales* and *Outstanding Walks Wales.*

The information in this book was accurate at the time of publication, but it can change at any time. Please confirm the details for the places you're planning to visit before you head out on your adventures.